Keepers of the Light

Portland Bill and Chance Glassworks

Brendan Jackson
with Geoff Broadway

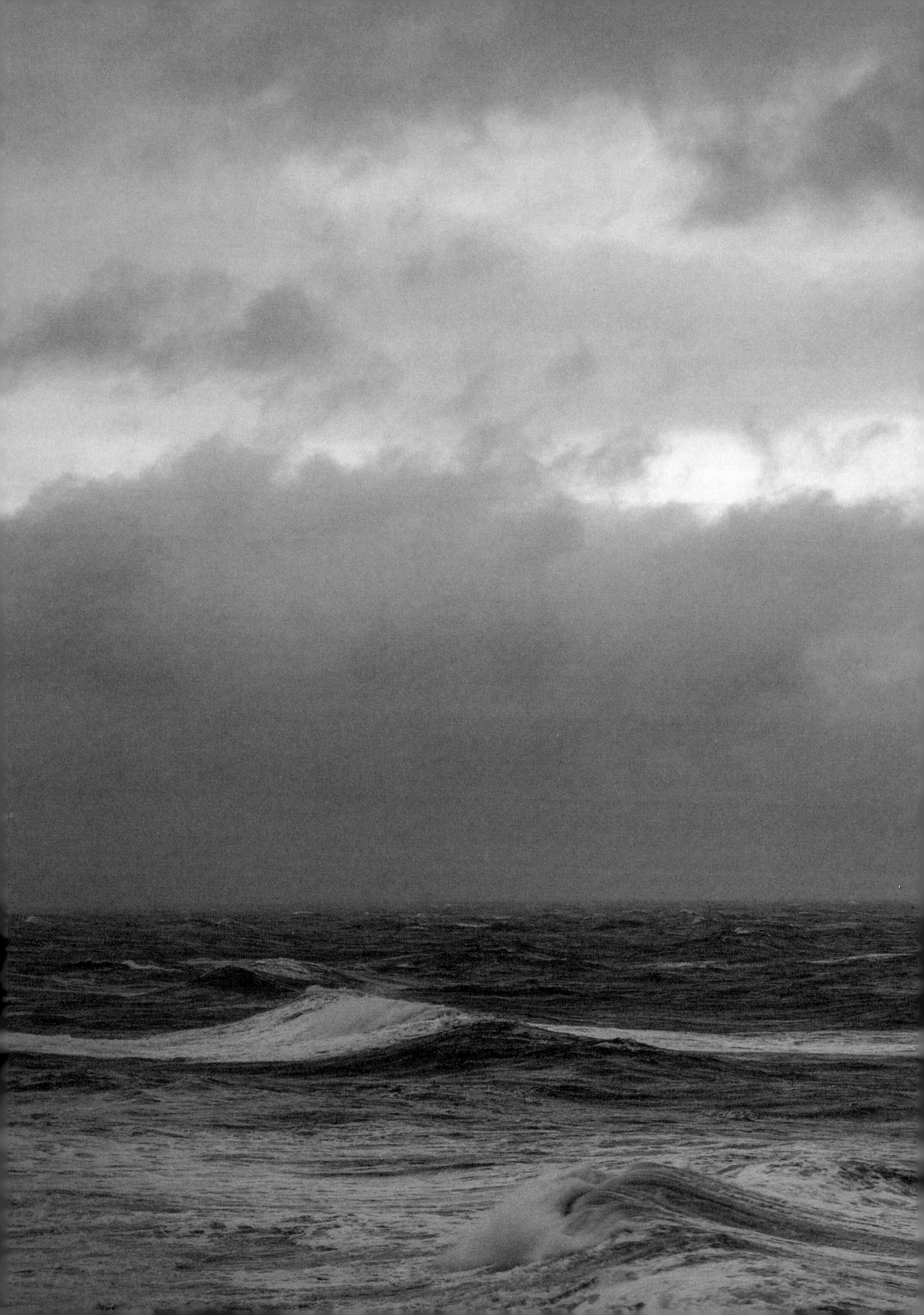

Bitter the winds that strike our coastal shore

And whip the sea to wrath

Yet colder still the rain

In anger swirling forth

- F. M. Ovendon, Dorset Year Book, 1955-56

About a week after
a French Brig

"came on Shore under Stone Cliff
and all her Crew perished her
Cargo was Turpentine Stocin Pitch
&c & just after that the Cliff fell
away just the W side of Walsend
gate and John Cumben was gain...
by under the said Cliff was
killed and buried and his remains
still lying there

THE following particulars are to hand concerning the wreck of the barque Lanoma in the English Channel on the 8th inst. : The iron clipper barque Lanoma, 665 tons, belonged to Messrs J. B. Walker and Co.'s line. She left Launceston on December 23, under the command of Captain T. B. Whittingham, with a crew of 18 hands all told, the first officer being Mr W. Cruse and the second officer Mr J. Fox. The cargo consisted of 5 tons 15cwt. ground bark, 245,027 sides of leather, 243lb Angora goat hide, 280 skins, 4 cases of beeswax, 15cwt. 1qr. of horns, 1 ton 5cwt. 3qr. shanks, 8cwt. 9lb. hair, 500 sheepskins, 1,083,650lb. wool. The total value of the cargo was £45,548 18s 6d. The Lanoma was built at Sunderland in 1877 by Messrs Austin and Hunter, and arrived at Launceston in the latter end of the same year, under the command of Captain W. R. Barwood, now harbour-master at Launceston. Whittingham, who was captain of the barque Araunah, of the same line, assumed command of the Lanoma in 1881, and ever since then has been trading from London to Launceston. Captain Whittingham married Miss Reading, of Launceston, and had nine children, all of whom are living. The Lanoma was a swift sailer, and one of the most popular vessels in the colonial merchant service. Both the vessel and cargo were well covered by insurance in various offices.

It was a dark and stormy night

Let's begin there, as so many stories have before. Out in Deadman's Bay, named for good reason, imagine your ship driven by the hard winds and rain toward the unseen shore. Tossed this way and that, the sea in constant sickening motion. Pitch black. The terrible roar of the gale and the toppling of huge waves, a frightful cacophony. The ship pitches and rolls, sails torn apart, hatches smashed, all too soon to be a hopeless mass of shattered wood on jagged rocks or shingle beach, cargo and crew spilled.

By day, in finer weather, you can see the long stretch of the Chesil Beach reaching towards the rugged stone island, a seemingly tenuous connection, the top of Portland rising up with its Victorian fortress, the land falling away southwards to the Bill, where our iconic lighthouse stands.

'Strictly speaking,' Christopher Stocks points out, 'it isn't an island at all, but what the French call a presqu'île, an almost-island.' This almost-Isle has been a Royal Manor since before the time of the Conqueror, sticking out into the English Channel like a pointed finger, with its own ways and customs, and unique geology.

The Channel might seem familiar, homely, picturesque, placid – less remarkable, as we cross it daily by car ferry, fly above it, or as we speed beneath it. One of the world's busiest shipping lanes, less impenetrable than it used to be, even swum by a children's author and comedian in $10\frac{1}{2}$ hours as he raises money for charity. Looks are deceptive. We can't see the hidden dangers.

Local historian Stuart Morris sets the scene: 'You've got all these powerful currents going up and down the Channel, meeting at Portland from both directions. Off the Bill there's a ledge, which is fairly deep – it's almost like an underwater promontory. It drops away very steeply, so when the tides flow over the ledges they boil up to the surface and create enormous turbulence, which is the famous – or infamous – Portland Race. That has always been a hazard. In the days of sail the number of ships lost there were legion. We'll never know how many vessels came to grief. I've read accounts of ships caught in the Race then suddenly swallowed up never to be seen again, men and cargoes there at the bottom somewhere.'

Apart from this strong tidal race and shallow reef, a few miles off the Bill there's a shoal called the Shambles Bank – only a few feet below the surface at low tide, over 3 miles long and 1 mile wide, the bottom continually moving and changing. Tom Cunliffe, author of the *Shell Channel Pilot*, describes this place around the Bill as 'the most dangerous extended area of broken water in the English Channel.'

Portland folk knew well the impact of the elements and the cost of shipping fatalities around their Isle. John Thomas Elliot of Weston kept a diary. Most of his daily entries start with a weather report.

> **4th January 1873.** A very strong wind veering from SSW to SW all day and a very thick rain. I was home in the morning making out the quarterly accounts. Went down to Weston in the afternoon. Portland Roads is nearly full of ships and vessels still going in. Some with their masts gone, some with bulwarks and some with cargo shifted. Nothing of consequence took place.

> **10th January 1873.** Wind about SW a steady brease fine all day. We worked all day and saw a steamer go up dismasted. She was well in the bay but it appeared that her engin was all right and she whent out if the bay. We could see though a glass one of the stumps of the mast and funnel.

> **26th February 1873.** Will and I & Harry got up about 1.30 in the morning and whent out the Beal and halled up the boat. The wind was S at that time. Come home and whent to bed again. Whent down in Will Otters Quarry in the morning and made three Roaches to make up a load and sent them away. Whent up lap yets after dinner and saw a barque sunk about a mile of Powell. Her crew got out in a boat and pulled up of Breston and then the Turk took them up and carried them to Weymouth. We whent over Church Hope to launch but never had enough hands. Her crew consisted of 8 men and a dog. Her name was the Ulverstone of Hull. She was laden with 350 tons of Coals & Coke. She was ran into by an Austrian Barque called the Concordia. She rendered no assistance to the Sinking Crew. She was stopped in Portland Roads by the Government. The Captain had a trial and was brought under £4000 damage. It is said the Ulverstone was only 63 years old.

At the end of his diary, Elliot also keeps a description of wrecks, many of which he has seen in his own lifetime. As he closes the final page, it is only 6 years since Chance Brothers installed the new lights in the Upper and Lower Lighthouses on Portland; at the glassworks in Smethwick they are now constructing lenses bound for Cape D'Aguilar in Hong Kong, for Heligoland, Port Adelaide in Australia, Aitidor in the Crimea, Poeloe Bars Island, Java, and South Stack Rock at Holyhead.

Blow wind, rise sea, ship 'shore 'fore day

In 1925 Hilaire Belloc describes his experience sailing past the Bill. He writes: 'There is no set of the sea in Portland Race; no run and sway; no regular assault. It is a chaos of pyramidical waters leaping up suddenly without calculation, or rule of advance. It is not a charge, but a scrimmage; a wrestling bout; but a wrestling bout of a thousand against one. It purposely raises a clamour to shake its adversary's soul, wherein it most resembles a gigantic pack of fighting dogs, for it snarls, howls, yells, and all of this most terrifically. It's purpose is to kill, and to kill with a savage pride.' He likens it to 'a huge pendant hanging from the tip of a demon's ear.' An infernal cauldron, in which vessels of all kinds have foundered on the rocks. Along this stretch of Dorset coast, over the past centuries so many have come to ruination. Among them:

A British troop transporter bound for the West Indies.
A French brig full of coffee and cotton.
A Swedish schooner laden with salt.
A Danish brig full of fruit.
A German steamer carrying oil.
A Dutch galliot full of oranges, tobacco and wine.
An English schooner carrying Welsh slate.
An Exeter brig carrying timber.
A Spanish brig with sugar and mahogany.
An Austrian pollacco, out of Trieste, a cargo of timber, cloth and sugar.

So many losses. A French barque taking 890 tons of coal from Dunkirk to Senegal is wrecked on Chesil Beach, as is a Latvian schooner carrying fireclay from Teignmouth to Lisbon; as is an East Indiaman on the last stretch of its voyage from Bombay to London, with a consignment of cotton, sugar, coffee, pepper and rice, only four Lascars and one woman passenger survive. An ironclad bound for Wellington, New Zealand, collides with a wooden ship bound for New York, with dreadful loss of life despite the best efforts of local fishermen attempting a rescue.

Down to the bottom goes barley from Ipswich intended for Glasgow, logs from St Domingo, cattle from New York, salt from Cadiz bound for Bergen, a cargo of iron pyrites from Huele intended for Rotterdam, coal and coke from South Shields destined for Carthagena, floorboards en route from Drammen to Dartmouth, wine and soap for Amsterdam, coal for Genoa. A cargo of deals going from Nardmaling to Nantes is lost, as is a cargo of matches, tar, turpentine and acid being taken from Hamburg to Buenos Aires. Ore from Sagunto never reaches Rotterdam, wool from Brisbane will never be unloaded at Liverpool docks. Roadstone and tin ingots from Newlyn lie scattered on the sea-bed.

It is only in 1852 that the Admiralty begin to collect statistics on shipping casualties, extending this in 1856 to include the causes of shipwrecks, as they recognise the problems of poor navigational aids at both harbours and along the shipping lanes. Three years later a Royal Commission is set up to examine all lighthouses around Britain and Ireland, as well as visiting those in France and Spain.

A brief history of the lighthouse

Born on the Isle, a civil engineer by profession, Stuart Morris has researched and published several fine books on local history, his interest stimulated by the discovery of his family's involvement with quarrying, fishing and smuggling. 'It's a true island community,' he says. 'No question about it. With its own ways, customs, folklore and pride too. You'll have a job to find a postcard of Portland that doesn't have a picture of the lighthouse.'

He describes to us how the Romans lit beacon fires on Branscombe Hill above the Bill (and they also introduced glassmaking skills to Britain), how two stone windmill towers near Wakeham did not provide satisfactory marks for navigation. He explains how there is a proposal to build a lighthouse in 1669 which comes to nothing, then in 1702 a petition is sent to the King by Charles Langrishe and Captain William Holman, supported by ship owners and Weymouth Corporation. They want a lighthouse on the southern tip of Portland, where it can be seen from both westerly and easterly approaches. They argue:

THAT the Isle of Portland shooteth out farr into the Sea to the Southward, and makes to great Bayes; commonly called the East and West bayes.

THAT by reason of its been farr in the Sea, the Tydes run with so great Impetuosity agt. the head land; that it makes very dangerous Race at some distance from the Island; but yett leaves room enough of Smooth Water in good weather, between the Race in the Island; for ships to sayl without danger in the daytime; though none dare venture in the Night; it being very narrow.

THAT sometimes, especially in Spring Tydes on Stormy Weather; the Sea runs so high in the Race that it's very dangerous ships (tho very great) to pass it; and much more for Small; and tis believed; that several Ships homeward bound that have been seen in the Channel; but never arriv'd at their Ports; have been there swallowed up; not knowing in the Night time how to avoid the Race; And Islanders have seen Several Ships sinck in Storms; but never Saw or heard of such Ships Goods or Men, or any part of their Wreck afterwards.

THAT a space to the Eastward of the Race is a Shoal; commonly called the Shambles on wch. at very low Tydes hath been found at (some) places not above 16 foot Water; which being known to very few Marriners; many for fear of it; anchor so near to the North shore; where there are Ledges of Rocks and foul

ground; that they are in great Danger and commonly loose (or at least Spoyl)
their Ground Tackle; as it happened to the Lenox and another Third Rate Ship
(in May 1702) bound for Ireland; who by the Accident were forced to leave off
their fflagg; and return to Portsmouth for Anchors.

The death of the King that year – along with recalcitrance from Trinity House to admit there is any hazard – keeps the petition in limbo for over a decade. Trinity House, evolving from a medieval mariner's guild, are the body authorised by Parliament (since 1566) to build 'such and so many beacons, signs and marks for the sea in such place or places of the seashore and uplands near the sea coasts or forelands of the sea whereby the dangers may be avoided and escaped and ships the better come unto the ports without peril.' Their full name is 'The Master, Wardens and Assistants of the Guild, Fraternity or Brotherhood of the most glorious and undivided Trinity and of St. Clement in the Parish of Deptford Strond, in the County of Kent.' Their charter includes compulsory pilotage of shipping and the exclusive right to licence pilots on the Thames. The Crown still retains the right to grant individuals the right to build a lighthouse, who charge fees to passing ships, in return for payment of rent.

The petitioners finally succeed; in 1716 two lighthouses are constructed, to give a clear bearing by day and night. They are coal-fired, powered by bellows. This fuel come from the Tyne, landed on Portland's east coast and hauled across rough ground to the lights, piled up in a field, which becomes known as Coal Lands. In 1752, overseers from Trinity House sail to Portland to make an inspection. They report: 'It was nigh two hours after sunset before any light appeared in either of the lighthouses' and that 'both lanterns are of a distressed state from the absence of polishing.' A few years later the Lower Lighthouse is given new equipment along with keepers' accommodation, which costs £1,000. At the same time the Higher Lighthouse is raised an additional 15 feet to increase its range.

When the lease is up for renewal it is refused and Trinity House take over running both lights. In 1788, they commission the installation of Argand lamps at the Higher Lighthouse, the first in Britain to be fitted with these illuminants; they consist of 14 lamps in two rows, each with a cotton wick enclosed in a glass tube which gives a clean, intense light, roughly ten times brighter than before. Highly polished metal reflectors help cast the light. The Lower Light also becomes the first lighthouse anywhere in the world to use magnifying lenses.

In 1844, Trinity House build a tall white stone obelisk on the tip of the Bill, as a warning of a low shelf of rock extending some 100 feet south into the sea. It is engraved simply with the letters T.H. and the date. In 1859, the first lightship is positioned on the Shambles. Three years later, Trinity House consider installing new electric lights at Portland, but the Elder Brethren are not yet convinced by field tests. Of Dungeness, which has one electric light on trial, they express dissatisfaction: 'Keepers hardly considered competent to take charge; extinguished 14th February; again exhibited, 6th June 1862.' James Douglass, their Engineer-in-Chief reports: 'Frequent extinctions of the light occurred from various causes connected with the machinery and apparatus, and the oil light had, at such times, to be substituted.' After lengthy correspondence it is decided 'under the circumstances, no other course to pursue than to leave the lights at Portland in their present state.' They believe the lights should be the most powerful available but the lantern housing is too small for this, so four years on they decide to demolish the two lights and completely rebuild. The new lights are operational in 1869; their buildings are whitewashed to be visible from the sea; both carry First Order lenses made by Chance Brothers of Smethwick.

In a terrible storm of 1901, the loss of some 14 ships near Portland prompts Trinity House to plan a completely new lighthouse. It is to be built on common land and compensation must be paid. In 1903, they negotiate with the Court Leet, local Committee of Commoners, to purchase the required land for £300, and in October Wakeham Bros. of Plymouth begin their preparatory work. On 2nd December that year, Chances write in their Order Book Number 12, in black ink: *'Portland Tower. Turn Service Room 180° with the exception of its floor, leaving the other parts the same as at present. As per drawing.'* This is the first mention of the new light; the same day they record orders for Bura Lighthouse in Mozambique, Double Island and Reef Lighthouses in Burma, Flat Island in Mauritius, for Dover Harbour and a manual foghorn for Kings Lynn Conservancy Board.

Foundations are dug deep into the rock, some of the stone quarried on the spot. Work starts on the keeper's house and the tower itself in May 1904, and the lantern is hoisted into place in late 1905. The light is lit on 11th January 1906 with 51-year-old Thomas Matthews on hand to oversee proceedings. Having joined Trinity House at the age of 25, he has held the position of Engineer-in-Chief since Douglass retired in 1892. As well as the new light here, he is responsible for the design of lighthouses, working closely with Chances, most recently at Pendeen (1900), Beachy Head (1902),

Foreland (1904) and Dungeness (1904). (He also designs a new type of incandescence oil burner, which is far more efficient than the concentric wick burner.) Principal Keeper William Taylor moves from the Lower Light (where he has served 4 years) to the new light. Richard Comben moves from his duties on the Portland Breakwater light to be his assistant. Comben will work here for the next five years, before going to Spurn Head; his family, old Portlanders, have provided keepers for the lights at the Bill over generations.

The tower is 134 feet tall. There are 153 steps to the top (two are added much later). The First Order lens weighs 3½ tons, 5 feet tall, made up of 4 separate lenses and a concave prismatic reflector. It sits on a doughnut shaped metal bath containing over half a ton of mercury. As they revolve, the glass prisms will give the Bill its signature – 4 white flashes every 20 seconds. It will reach out 25 nautical miles. A red sector light is provided in addition to the main light, which shines from a window lower down the tower, to indicate the position of The Shambles. The lighthouse costs £13,000 to build, when you can buy at this time a 3-bedroom house in Mayfair for £600.

The redundant lighthouses are auctioned. Stuart Morris tells us they were advertised as: 'Wonderfully suited for consumptives in winter, and convalescents in other seasons. In the fertile garden of the Lower Lighthouse potatoes are dug when people elsewhere are thinking of planting.' The Higher Light sells for £405 and is later purchased in 1923 by Marie Stopes, a controversial pioneer of family planning and women's rights. By the time of the Great War, the Lower Light becomes for a time Longstone Ope Tea Rooms and Gardens, with an observation point where the lens used to be. A stone tablet from the Lower Light is retained. It is fixed above the entrance to the new tower, on the ground floor, where the engines of compressed air that operate the fog horn stand. Part of the inscription reads:

For The Direction and Comfort of NAVIGATORS;
For The Benefit and Security of COMMERCE;
And For A lasting Memorial of BRITISH HOSPITALITY
To All Nations

As technological marvel and as an observer of changing times, if only the light could speak, what stories might it tell of treacherous currents, of safe passage, of trade and travel, of the condition of our island nation, of our industriousness and sense of place?

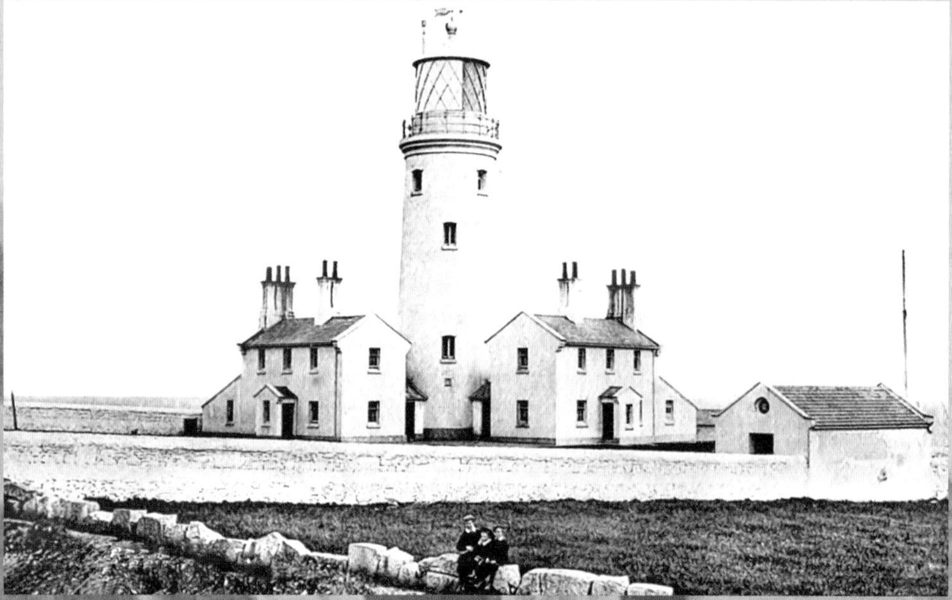

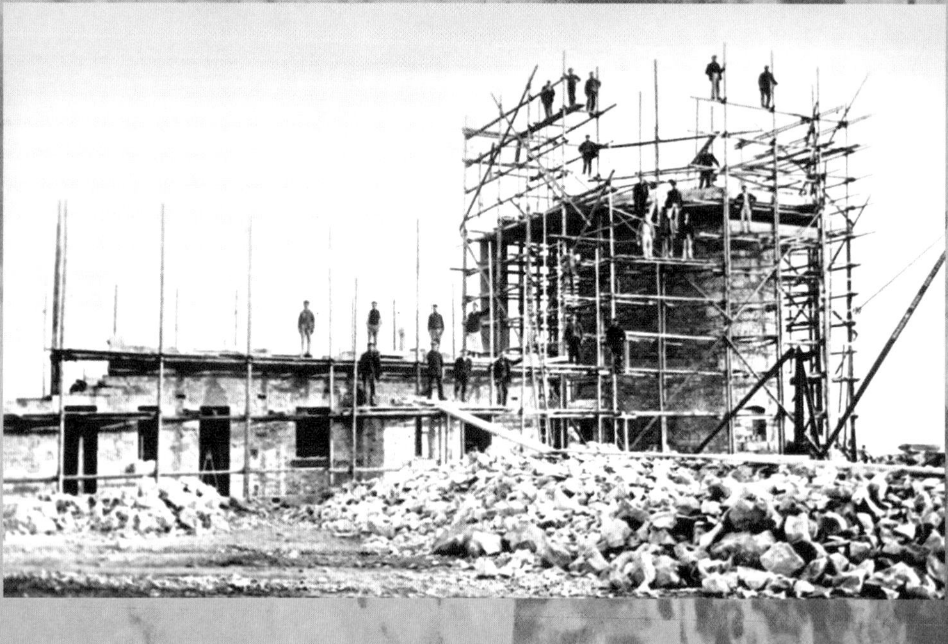

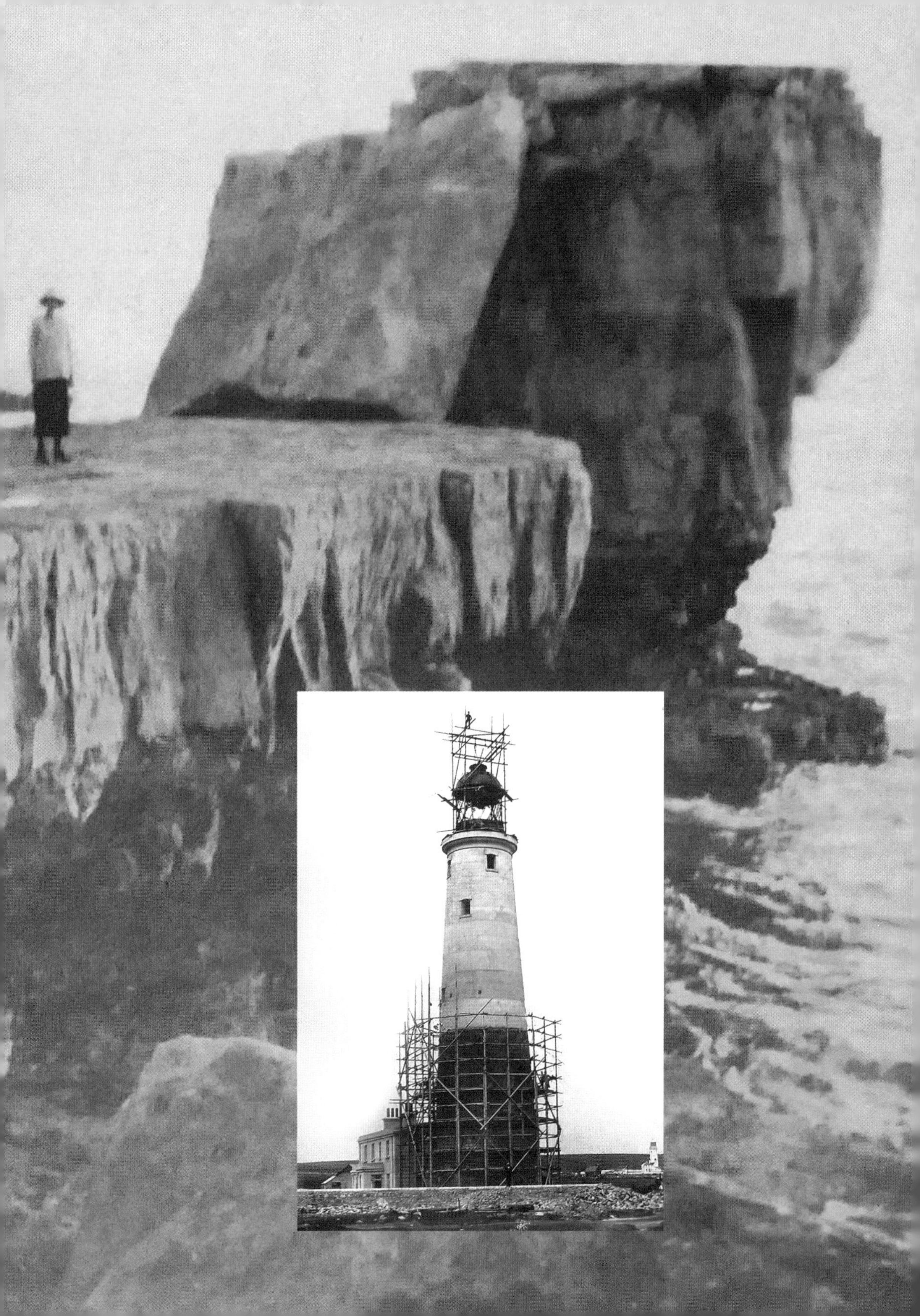

Handwritten entries from Chances Order Book

6th January 1904. Portland Lantern. Trinity House have no templates for the glass for above; it will, therefore, be necessary for us to make these.

28th September 1904. Trinity House. For Portland Bill Lighthouse. Lantern of 14 feet diameter, similar to those supplied for Pendeen and the Foreland, but pedestal to be 4' - 9" high, to Trinity House printed specification. No glazing to be supplied. Trinity House will supply the roof ventilator, with the exception of the Vane work, which we are to supply. Our contract includes the delivery and erection at site. By 27 May 1905 eight months. *Added in red ink:* Price £1125 less allowance from ventilator. *Added in pencil:* Penalty for delay 20/- per day. 8/4/05 No blanking to be supplied.

19th October 1904. Trinity House. For Portland Bill Lighthouse. Dioptric apparatus of 920 m/m focal distance (with upper and lower prisms) consisting of one group of flashing panels, backed by Dioptric mirror having a vertical angle of 100°, for giving four white flashes, each of .17 second, separated by an eclipse of 1.4 second, at periods of 20 seconds. (The focal plane will be 140 feet above H.W.O.S.T, note added 21/10/04). Pedestal bearings, with mercury float but without mercury. Clockwork. Note! The burner to be used will be the single mantle 'Matthews' incandescent oil burner. In 10 months from 13th Oct 04 without fail. (13th August 1905). *Added in red ink:* £2171-0-6. Plus extra for delivery to site of lighthouse.

21st October 1904. Portland Bill Lighthouse apparatus. The available fall for driving weight is 13 feet, less the length of the weights and pulleys. The focal plane will be 140 feet above H.W.O.S.T.

22nd October 1904. For Portland Bill. They are sending us a copper roof ventilator, which is to be fixed to the roof of the lantern for Portland Bill.

13th December 1904. Trinity House. For Portland Bill. Repair damaged roof ventilator.

9th January 1905. Mr. Matthews writes under date 6/1/1905, as follows: 'With reference to the service stage, please have it filled in solid, as I arranged with Mr. Robson yesterday.'

31st March 1905. Portland Bill. Sufficient mercury to be supplied to float the apparatus, & 10% as spare.

3rd April 1905. For Portland Bill lantern. No blanking will be required for the above lantern.

May 4th 1905. Copy of letter from Mr. Matthews 3/5/05. Portland Bill. 'I will arrange to have Lantern inspected on 3rd please expedite matters by proceeding with making packing cases.'

May 13th 1905. Trinity House. "Portland Bill Lantern. Please have the holding down bolts ready to be dispatched with the above."

July 8th 1905. Portland Bill Apparatus. The above must be ready for inspection by Mr. Matthews on July 31st (Monday).

August 26th 1905. Portland Bill Low Light. Under date of 25th August Mr. Matthews writes to us as follows: "With further reference to the question of the ruby shades for the Low Light, window frames for which you have kindly put aside on one of my late visits to your works, please prepare 6 of these, carefully pack & send them to Mr. W. Williams at the lighthouse as soon as possible. They are to be cut and bent to a template which is being forwarded to you. The radius of the inner face is 9' 6", height 3' 3 7/8", and the thickness 3/8."

Jan 16th 1906. Letter from Mr. Matthews on 15th. Portland Bill. Replace broken prism i.e. the fourth from the top. Supply necessary materials for the fixing.

The era of magnificence

If only you could decipher them, like petrologists, paleontologists and stratigraphers can do, what a story the rocks of Portland would tell, as they are quarried, chipped, knapped, split apart. Scratch beneath the surface and uncover a story of millions of years past, what creatures lived then, preserved in the sedimentary rock long before humans set foot here, this limestone and chert from the Tithonian period. The Domesday Book records the presence on the Isle of one villager, 90 smallholders, 5 slaves, 3 Lord's ploughing teams, 23 men's ploughing teams, 3 cobs, 14 cattle, 27 pigs, 900 sheep, 8 acres of meadow, 8 furlongs of pasture – value to the Lord (who was also the King) £65.

Smethwick at the time of the Domesday survey had 60 villagers and 22 smallholders recorded, with 52 acres of meadow, 1 mill, land enough to be worked by 7 Lord's ploughing teams and 22 men's ploughing teams, all part of the Manor of Lichfield. The geology hereabouts in the Black Country will later offer up the base materials needed for glassmaking. The diversity of mineral wealth lying beneath our feet includes coal, ironstone, limestone, fireclay and brick clays, sand and gravel, which give rise to the major manufacturers of the Industrial Revolution.

A few years into the 20th century, Smethwick has the appearance of a relatively prosperous industrial town. No one calls its architecture beautiful but civic leaders feel it has a character in keeping with local industry, concerned with practical rather than artistic ideals. A new town hall is under construction on the High Street. The arms of the borough from 1899 to 1907 are quartered to represent various industry in the town, showing a pumping engine, a lighthouse, a gasholder, a worker at an anvil; their motto, *Orbis terrarum officina*. It has some pleasant Victorian town houses, though the housing stock is mostly terraces, those we call two-up two-downs. Conversion of their privies into water closets is underway, along with the abolition of middens; 3,000 middens will be gone by 1907 and nearly 4,500 water closets provided. The streets of the borough are well paved. For the growing population, new estates are being planned. Shopkeepers are adopting electric lighting; suppliers promise 'No damage to Goods or Decorations, No Steaming of windows, No fouling of Atmosphere.'

There is a new electric tram service from Oldbury to Birmingham, via Smethwick, with a tram every few minutes from Windmill Lane and every 10 minutes from Spon Lane. The service begins at 4.45 am and runs until

11.30 pm. There are some gas explosions in conduits on the high street in connection with the trams, which Alderman Pinkney has personally observed. The cause is put down to some sparks from leakage of electricity, rather than vagrant coal gas. There are complaints about the timing of the trams, particularly with the 30-minute services, as 19 out of 20 trams are missing the connection at the Cape; the trams are also overloaded and people compelled to stand up, women and children obliged to ride outside in the cold. There are protests about the noise of trams as they pass over the points, residents saying they cannot sleep because of the racket.

The town has several public parks and recreation grounds. West Smethwick Park, some 50 acres of former farmland purchased by Sir James Timmins Chance (who recently passed away), was presented to the town in 1895 for public benefit. Here the foliage is abundant and the displays organised by the park keeper, Mr Driver, are tastefully laid out. Though the prevalence of chemicals in the air is not favourable to the growth of trees, he has done an excellent job but despairs of any great success with regard to arboriculture. He welcomes the easterly winds, as they carry the chemicals in the opposite direction. Throughout the season, the parks offer music concerts with champion military and brass bands, and Pierrot performances. Cricketers play on the green. Up to 300 people turn up for a dip in the lake on Sunday mornings. According to Dr Jackson, the Medical Officer, in his 1904 report to the town council, the parks 'afford exceptionally healthy playing grounds for young children, and are, besides being a great attraction to the neighbourhood, a valuable feature for the promotion and preservation of health.'

The population of Smethwick is an estimated 61,000, who occupy 13,160 houses. 1,956 children are born, 45 illegitimate. Dr Jackson reports that marriage is in decline. He notes: 'This decrease in the community where there are so many young people of marriageable age is very striking. No doubt it is partly attributable to the general slackness of trade that has obtained, but other influences whose extent it is difficult to appraise with any accuracy, have doubtless being an appreciable contributory cause of it.' There are 810 deaths recorded; 59 over the age of 5 died of phthisis, 49 of cancers, 76 of bronchitis, 86 of pneumonia; 285 children under 12 months died. Personal and domestic cleanliness were often wanting, he declares, stressing the need to be continually vigilant over insanitary conditions in the dwellings of the large working class population. With 17 slaughterhouses, 11 cowsheds, 125 dairies and milkshops in the borough, no infectious diseases are traced to the use of local milk. The waterworks maintain their reputation for purity. 'One of the most important means for the maintenance of health in the Borough,' says the Doctor, 'has no doubt been the exceptionally excellence of the water.'

Health concerns dominate local advertisements in newspapers and street hoardings. The chemist on the High Street, H. M. Tranmer, offers a cure for the 'winter of discontent' – their Cream Emulsion of Cod Liver Oil is made from the finest oil in Norway and they commend it to medical parctitioners for those with weak lungs and chest, for children with whooping cough and 'all those who are sufferers of Cold Feet and Hands should try a short treatment with this Emulsion. It imparts more heat to the body than a complete suit of woollen clothes.'

Having attended a meeting at the Smethwick Recreative and Athletic Association to hear Dr Stanley Barnes lecture on the subject of *The Heart* and the value of exercise (though he does not advocate too much, as it can

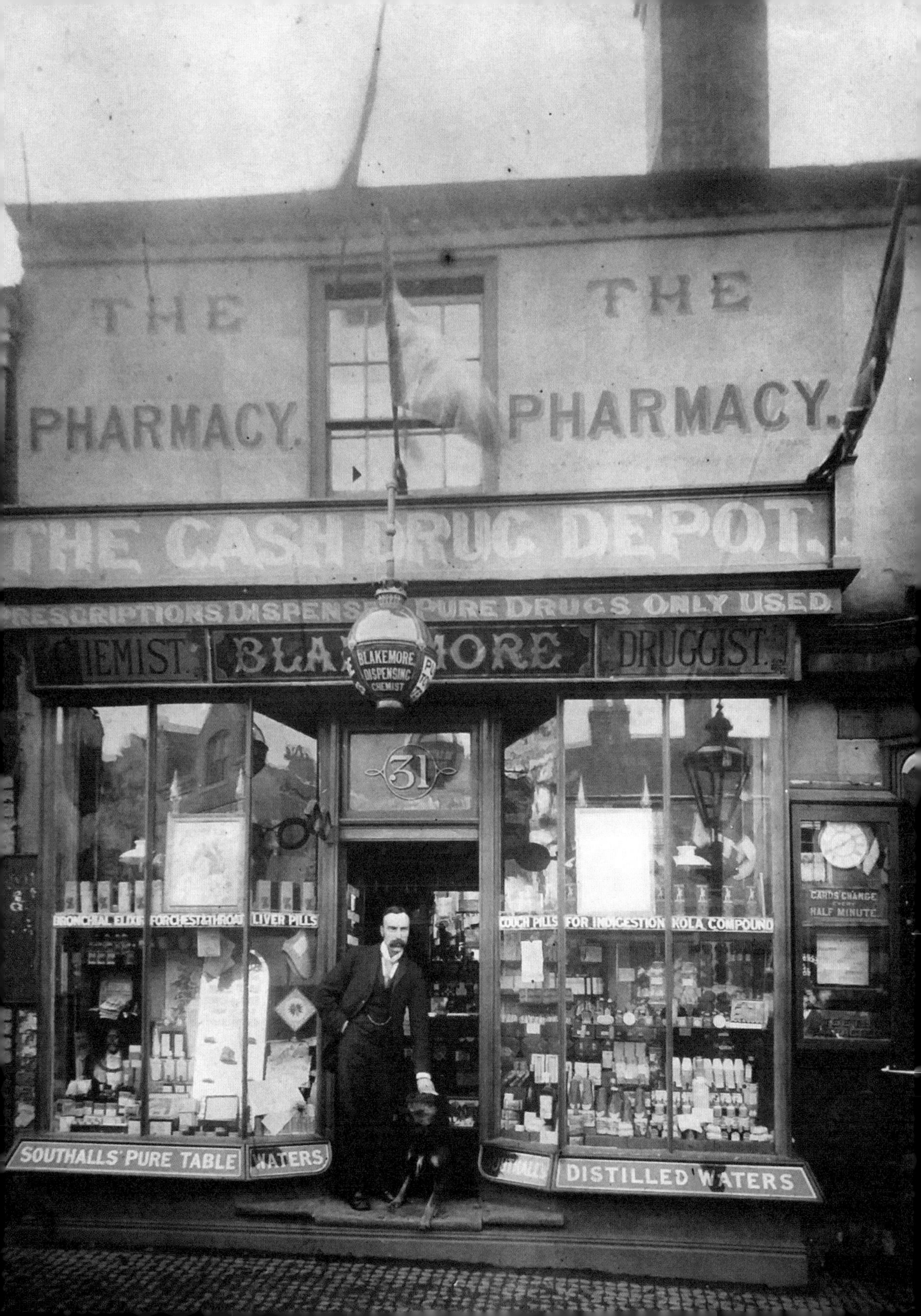
THE PHARMACY.
THE PHARMACY.
THE CASH DRUG DEPOT.
PRESCRIPTIONS DISPENSED PURE DRUGS ONLY USED.
CHEMIST
BLAKEMORE
DRUGGIST
BLAKEMORE DISPENSING CHEMIST
31
BRONCHIAL ELIXIR FOR CHEST & THROAT LIVER PILLS
COUGH PILLS FOR INDIGESTION KOLA COMPOUND
CARDS CHANGE EVERY HALF MINUTE
SOUTHALLS' PURE TABLE WATERS
DISTILLED WATERS

place undue strain on that organ), as well as telling of the perils of the 'tobacco heart' and excess amounts of alcohol (all impressively illustrated by means of lime-light views), a glass worker of 1905 might then notice a series of advertisements in the Smethwick Telephone, which extol the virtues of Dr Williams' Pink Pills for Pale People, an iron-rich blood tonic available over the counter. One tells the story of Mr Charles Vosper of Dorset, a carpenter by trade and a keen amateur athlete whose walking has won him some degree of fame. He is suffering from depression and languor; he no longer relishes his meals, he feels weak and his legs tremble. Something is wrong with him, which he put down to the effects of a cold, but the condition persists. He loses a stone in weight and he no longer has any appetite for races. However, he soon regains his vigour after a course of the marvellous Pink Pills. Our glass worker might not realise that Mr Vosper will soon be able to walk from the Verne to Portland Bill and back again to West Weares in tremendous good spirit – and perhaps even have the pep for some labouring at the keeper's house which is now taking shape there, alongside the rising stone body of the tower, as the prisms themselves are being carefully prepared here in the glassworks.

The Gospel Hall at Cape Hill offers a Bible Class for men and women and a talk by Mr A. J. Gasking on *A Model Wife*. At St Michael's Church, *Christ the Socialist* is the topic of an address given by Reverend Archer, who states that a Socialist works for the regeneration of society, of morals and the arts, on the basis of a community of interests and of cooperation of labour for the common good. Socialism some 50 years ago may have been associated with violence, but there were periods in the Church's history also connected with violent acts; the true Socialist, he concludes, whether he professes Christianity or not, follows in the footsteps of Christ.

It is the opinion of some that local folk are not particularly enamoured of lectures unless they happen to be 'in lighter vein.' However, Reverend E. Lloyd Jones attracts 200 people to his lecture on *Oliver Cromwell and Puritan Ideals*. The Smethwick Institute presents *Irish Life and Song* by Miss O'Connor, while over at the Town Hall, Special War Correspondent Mr Walter Kirton narrates his experiences with the Japanese Army at the front. Admission is 6d, side galleries and front of floor, 1s, great gallery, 2s; proceeds are divided between the Smethwick District Nursing Association, the Police-aided Association for Clothing Destitute Children and Smethwick Aid Society.

At Smethwick Women's Liberal Association, they discuss the burning topic of *Women's Suffrage*. The prospective Liberal candidate Herbert Leon sends a letter of apology, stating that he is in favour of giving the vote to women and furthermore would not confine it only to women of property. (Smethwick is still part of the Handsworth Constituency until 1918, when Handsworth will be incorporated into the city of Birmingham). Miss Southall, secretary of the Birmingham Women's Liberal Association is cordially welcomed to Smethwick even though she is said to be 'coming from such a politically dark place as Birmingham.' Miss E. Finey speaks vigorously in favour of not only one-man one vote but of one-women one vote. She argues that in Smethwick there are a great many women wage earners who work to maintain their homes and perform just as laborious toil as men. She solicits loud applause.

Lighter entertainment may be found at the Theatre Royal in Rolfe Street. Open now for 8 years, it claims to be one of the largest theatres in the country, with over 3,000 seats. The Building News and Engineering Journal describes it most favourably; it has upholstery 'of dark red velvet plush, which forms a fine contrast with the tints employed in the general decorations, which consist for the most part of a very pale blue and a delicate rose pink, with a lavish admixture of gold. The whole of the woodwork is covered by most artistically wrought plastic decorations.' It attracts the best London companies. The stage is nearly 80 feet wide and 60 feet deep. There are 8 dressing rooms for the artists as well as a large chorus dressing room in the basement, each with a lavatory. The theatre, mostly lit with new electric light, is situated in the very centre of the town, opposite a rail station with trams running within a few yards of its doors. It is well within walking distance of the glassworks. The theatre boxes cost 10s and 6d, circle and stall, 1s and 6d, the Pit 6d, the gallery 4d. Worth every penny.

Frederick Melville's play *The Ugliest Woman on Earth* arrives in town, promoted as 'an original play of Extraordinary Interest,' a melodrama with a dangerous woman as the lead character, encouraging audiences to clap, cheer, boo and hiss. Melville likes to cast physically robust women in the lead roles, in working class settings. *A Sailor's Sweetheart* proves another popular play with patrons, with a 'charming story, full of exciting meetings, tender romance, irresistible humour, touching pathos, those factors so dear to the majority of local patrons'; it also features a Naval band. *At War with Women* is a comedy about a 'women's schemes and the trials of virtue' with thrilling scenes set in Russia and Paris. *The Voice of the People* is set nearby, in the world of Birmingham sweatshops, featuring women exploited by a ruthless charmer but redeemed by high-minded social reformers. The Smethwick

Telephone offers a little dissent, asking if there is a growing dislike of titles of these plays and their unashamed presentation on hoardings, which 'may offend the casual passerby.' They write: 'Often the title is the greatest advertisement, but lately we are afraid the names of some of the dramas have been sufficient to keep many away altogether.' They hope that in future the theatre will offer some more tasteful fare, suggesting promenade concerts with a prominent vocalist. One portent of the future is already here; between acts, audiences are treated to 'an exceptional extra attraction' – they are entranced by 'Animated Pictures' whose titles include *The Unlucky Birthday Umbrella*, *A Cruiser in a Storm*, *The Bombardment of Port Arthur*, *Great Irish Eviction Scene*, *Desperate Poaching Affray*, *The Blacksmiths Daughter*.

In the summer season, Victoria Park offers Sunday and weekday concerts – the first performed by the Royal Staffordshire Blues Band. Their repertoire includes Gladiator (Sousa), Le Minstrel (Lamottee), Hymn of Praise (Mendelssohn), and excerpts from Lucrezia Borgia (Donizetti). Stonemasons are putting the final touches to a drinking fountain in West Smethwick Park in memory of John Homer Chance – who has recently died – with funds raised from the workers at Chances. Another member of the Chance family, Alexander Macombe Chance, owner of Chance and Hunt, is lobbying to purchase the grounds of Warley Abbey as a public park. He recently helped saved Lightwoods Park from housing development. At a meeting at The Bear Hotel, speaking in support of the idea, Bishop Gore of Birmingham expresses the opinion that the country has been involved in a disastrous experiment in their cities which rational men should seek to reverse. He speaks movingly of the 'moral degradation and deterioration upon men and women when they were deprived of the power to look upon open spaces, the sense of distance, the knowledge of the country this deprivation of open spaces in cities, the spectacle of normal growth, singing of birds, free vision of the sky, and the open horizon.'

So Alexander Chance invites thousands to make their wishes known by visiting the grounds of Warley Abbey on the first August Bank Holiday Monday. He has already raised over £10,000 but more is now needed. He declares: 'The final decision rests with the workingmen. It is for them we are working, for them and their children forever. At our very doors this park exists. Let this opportunity slip, and the builder will soon obliterate forever one of Nature's most lovely gifts.' Indeed, many do come to the Abbey, although in the morning a drenching downpour of rain catches them out. A stream of visitors wander through the mud in the afternoon, Mr Chance

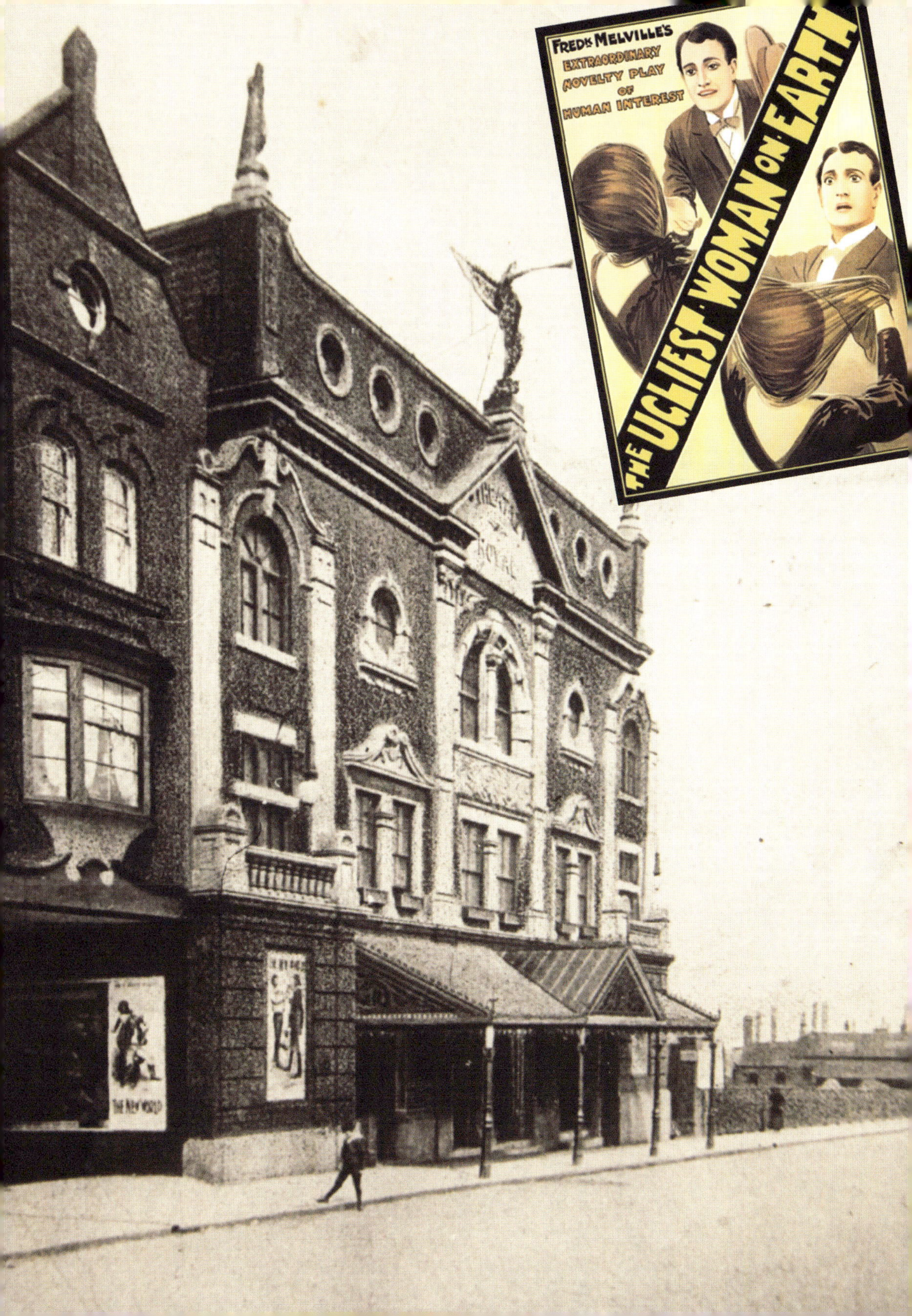
FREDK MELVILLE'S
EXTRAORDINARY
NOVELTY PLAY
OF
HUMAN INTEREST
THE UGLIEST WOMAN ON EARTH

chatting amiably with them, in between making announcements from a waggon which serves as an improvised platform. He appeals for more funds by public subscription to buy the park – 'a few thousand pounds to secure the deal, less than a farthing in the pound to everyone.'

While he also hopes for a contribution of £1,000 from Smethwick Council, he worries that some people have 'cramped ideas, those men who seemed too small for their own clothes,' those who do not believe they should support the project from the rates. He contends they need to be educated in how to give – there should be a special class of instruction given to those who could afford to give but would not and he states he would like to be the schoolmaster. He asks: 'Would Smethwick be disgraced forever, or would they retrieve their character?' The park is eventually purchased, though the Council is not inclined to increase the rates, saying the park is outside their area and they have a capital park already within their jurisdiction. One commentator argues: 'The prosperity of Smethwick and its working class are so dependent on its large works that every effort should be made to keep the rates low. The experience of neighbouring towns, whose high rates have driven manufacturers away is before us. The warnings from steelworks managers and railway directors should be heeded. Rigid economy is Smethwick's only safe policy.' (Some 20 years later the Council will admit to it being 'a most agreeable retreat on a summers day.')

There are Smethwick folk who choose not to visit Warley Abbey, but travel instead to Edgbaston Reservoir on the Monday, where among the many attractions are the Emerald Minstrels, who offer 'plantation songs' –

Come down, Gabriel, blow your horn
Call me home in the early morn'
Send the chariot down this way
Come and haul me home to stay
Angels meet me at the crossroads, meet me
Angels meet me at the crossroads, meet me
Angels meet me at the crossroads, meet me
Don't charge a sinner any toll

Heavy rain interrupts the merriment of the evening illuminations and the water carnival, people running for shelter in the skating rink. At Lightwoods Park there is a decent crowd to hear the Northfield Band playing. Victoria Park is deserted on Monday, even though several improvements have been publicised, the avenues of trees planted the previous year coming along nicely, the borders and flowerbeds adding charm to the scenery. However, there has recently been some wanton destruction of the flowers and foliage, which gives the park keeper, Mr W. Powell, considerable trouble and anxiety. Many other folk choose to travel to the seaside for a much needed change of scenery and air. In the small hours of the Friday morning, 10,000 people go to the coast. The rail platforms are thronged, the porters struggling with the amount of luggage but there no mishaps and no delays. One fifth are heading to Blackpool, though Bournemouth and Southampton are now vying for popularity, requiring two trains, whereas the year before they were not even on the list. Scarborough has dropped in popularity. The longest journeys are to Torquay and Plymouth. More people than ever are taking these trips. The holiday offers are tempting – up to a week in a resort for a few shillings a ticket.

Some factories have allowed workers to leave on Friday evening, overtime being worked on two evenings to account for the Saturday. Most are due back to work Wednesday morning. The railway companies lay on an extra 20 special trains to take the trippers. The Great Western can can take you to Taunton, Exeter, Dawlish, Teignmouth, Torquay, Plymouth, Builth Wells, Rhayader, Machynlleth, Glandovey, Borth, Aberystwyth, Aberdovey, Towyn, Barmouth, Llangollen, Shrewsbury, Worcester and Malvern. The London and North-Western line deposits holidaymakers at Blackpool, Rhyl, Colywn Bay, Llandudno, Scarborough, Penmaenmawr, Llanfairfechan, Bangor, Caernarvon, Llanberis, Liverpool, the Isle of Man and London. The Bay of Weymouth is not yet tempting folk from the Black Country.

A local innovation is pronounced a success – a scheme to take poor children for a day out, with 600 'street robins' (two thirds who are orphans) visiting Sutton Park, thanks to a 'fresh air fund' raised by local workers. Myra Horton and Annie M. Heath of The Firs, Smethwick, also launch a campaign, on behalf of The Soldiers and Sailors Association, to relieve the plight of the wives, widows and mothers of soldiers and sailors in 'troublesome times.' They appeal for donations, highlighting the needs of those on their books: a soldier who suffers from consumption, with only 5 shillings allowed his wife for a year; a soldier crippled through rheumatic fever, help given to his widowed mother; help given to the wife of a soldier in South Africa, with her three children fallen ill with the fever, one of whom has now died; help offered to the widow and children of a soldier who had died in India, to aid her find employment.

At the other end of the spectrum, a 67-year-old woman is called before the magistrates for stealing a ribbon that fastened a memorial card to a wreath upon a grave. She asks for leniency as magistrates express their 'disgust and chagrin' at such an action; she is fined £1 1s 6d and costs, or by default will spend seven days in prison. The court records give an indication of the moral climate, and social concerns and issues. To the shame of the townsfolk, several serious matters are passed on to Stafford Quarter sessions. One man is convicted of stealing cigars and pipes, a greengrocer is found guilty of embezzling funds from a colleague; both are sentenced to 12 months. A member of the local militia, John Shaw, aged 21, is charged with stealing a hearth rug worth 6s 6d from outside a draper shop at Christmas. He claims he was 'very drunk' but admitted he took it home and sold it for 2s and 6d – he gets 1 month. Two men, a riveter and a polisher, have stolen a violin, and get 6 months. A labourer who had stolen money gets 18 months. An 18-year-old soldier who broke into a shop is bound over for 6 months.

The local magistrates themselves are kept busy. Traders are lobbying police to clamp down on unthinking smokers because of the damage caused by the striking of matches on their shop fronts and doors of houses. Those who ought not even to be smoking are pointed out as the worst offenders. There has also been a considerable outbreak of stone-throwing damage to windows in the Cape Hill area. Eight boys are brought to court for these activities, having been arrested at Brookes Factory doing malicious damage, their parents claiming they have never caused any trouble. A 13-year-old girl from Rolfe Street is charged with stealing 1½ pence from the till of a local shopkeeper. She claims innocence, saying that she had put the money back before she was apprehended. Another 13 year-old girl, from Tat Bank, is charged with stealing brewery coal from a canal wharf; when taken into custody she said her Mother would kill if she went home without any.

Several boys from West Smethwick, aged 12 and 13, are charged with 'interfering with the comfort of railway passengers.' After a series of complaints about boys annoying schoolgirls on the railway, the London and North-Western Rail Company press charges. In one case a 10-year-old girl catches the 5'o'clock train with three other girls, when a gang of boys enters their compartment. The ringleader seizes her leg, pulls off her shoe, and pushes her to the floor, while the other boys restrain her friends. At Soho station, the boys let them go. The magistrates agree this conduct is a nuisance to be stopped but, because of the age of those involved, do not press a conviction on this occasion.

Meanwhile, three Birmingham girls 'typical of the class who parade the streets, wearing hair in curling pins, and maintaining a don't care appearance'

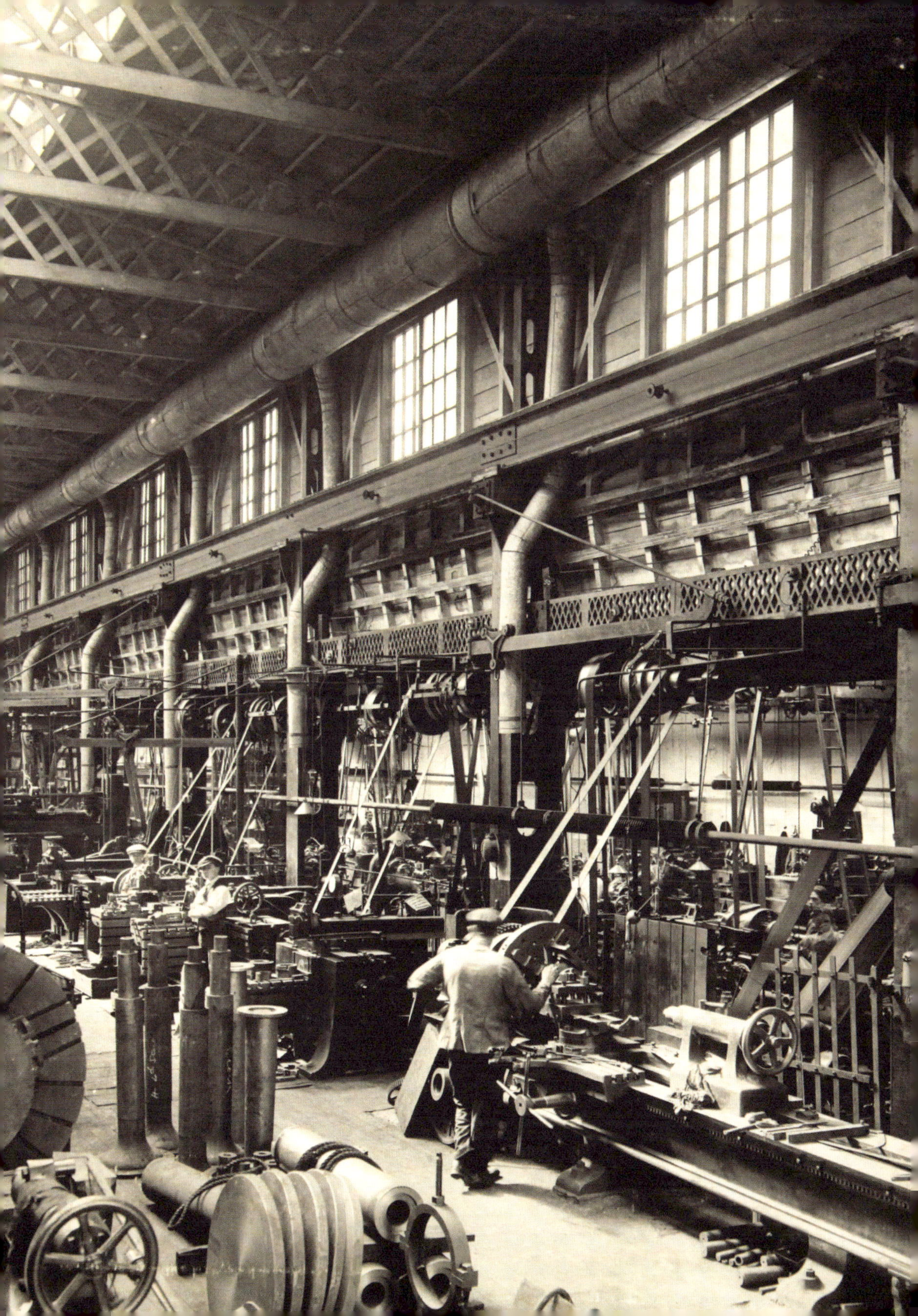

are placed in the dock on a charge of theft. Amy Gill (17), Rose Freeth (17) and Nellie Lovell (14) are charged with stealing a skirt worth 2s 9d from the shop of Mr Blackstaffe, a pawnbroker on Cape Hill. Gill and Lovell are also charged with stealing a pair of boots from a shop on Spring Hill. Gill says they were hungry and thought they might make a little money by pawning the boots, but because they were odd ones they did not. Freeth is given the benefit of the doubt and discharged. Gill, who has previously convictions, receives 1 month imprisonment with hard labour for each charge. Lovell is fined 10s and £1 in costs.

John Banks, along with Fred Duggins, a greengrocer of the High Street, is summoned for cruelly ill-treating a horse lame in two legs, by working it whilst in an unfit state. Two vendors are charged with hawking music in the Cape Hill area without a licence. A sailor is arrested for suspicious behaviour. It's a sorry tale he tells – invalided out the Navy due to consumption, rejoining under another name, found out and charged with false enlistment, then in trouble for burglary. He is sent to jail for a month, though not sentenced to hard labour because of his ill state. Another sailor, Henry Williams, aged 26, of no fixed abode, is charged with stealing a box of Woodbine cigarettes, value 3s 4d, from a shop on Shireland Road. He ran away, only to be arrested by Birmingham Police en route to Glasgow. He is fined 10s and 19d costs.

Mary Evans, aged 50, appears in a dual role, as defendant in charge of drunkenness and as complainant under the Married Woman's Act. She has already made some 30 appearances before the court due to states of inebriation. Her husband is summoned for desertion. They married in 1882 in County Cork and had 13 children. She asks for a separation order and a payment from her husband. In his defence he claims that her drunken habits led her that very morning to sell furniture for 9d and spend the proceeds on booze. Nevertheless, an order of 2s and 6d is granted to her. Edwin Mills of Montague Road is summoned for using abusive language towards Rose Whitehouse during a disturbance. She is a married woman whose husband has left her and argues that that the language used must be challenged in court, because if not it would damage her character and she may be dismissed from her workplace. He is fined 20s and 12d costs or face 14 days imprisonment.

John Crabbe, aged 38, of Unett Street, is summoned for persistent cruelty to his wife. It is claimed he had thrown the cat at her, then a lamp. The magistrates judge that it cannot be termed persistent cruelty as defined by the Act, as this had only taken place in the course of one day. His wife demands a separation and defamation of character. As the couple are young, the magistrates feel they ought to make an effort to live together and dismiss the case.

Local tradesmen express concerns of the scarcity of money and the growing ranks of the unemployed. The stone breaking yards for the relief of the unemployed remains open over the summer. They worry that the government is doing little for the economy, with food prices rising. The Smethwick Telephone notes this is 'a time when the unfortunate toiler seeks to try his fortunes abroad, and when the fortunate man turns his ambitions towards greater rewards.' They call for emigration information to be made widely available in the Free Library and Reading Rooms, so that the town may better contribute to the ranks of future colonists, and that emigrants may be better prepared in seeking their fortunes. While Canada wants farm labourers, where inexperience is not a disadvantage and they offer free board and lodging, New South Wales has no need for mechanics, miners or farm labourers but wants to recruit domestic servants. Tasmania and New Zealand do not offer any opportunities. As for South Africa, no one is allowed to land in Cape Colony unless he or she already has employment or possesses £20 on arrival. Recent settlers on farms are reported to be in difficulties owing to drought, locusts and their own inexperience.

The year of 1905 in Smethwick ends with electioneering. The Liberal opposition campaigns with the slogan: 'What Toryism means: South Africa for the Chinese; Faulty Rifles for Our Soldiers; Ratepayers money for Sectarian Schools; Doles for their Friends; Taxes for the Working Man; Dear Food for Everybody.' Locally, they say the miserable scale of teacher salaries has 'left people in the doldrums' and must be addressed.

Nationally the Liberals take power in a landslide victory in January 1906, the coalition of the Conservative Party and Liberal Unionists losing half their seats in Parliament. But in Smethwick, Mr Leon, the Liberal candidate, loses to the Liberal Unionist candidate, Ernest Meysey Thompson, who gets 60.8% of the vote, retaining the seat held previously by his father. In his campaign Thompson is opposed to Home Rule for the Irish; he states he is firmly an Imperialist and 'an enemy of the timid and short-sighted policy of the Little England faction' as well as being both a social reformer and a tariff reformer in favour of free trade.

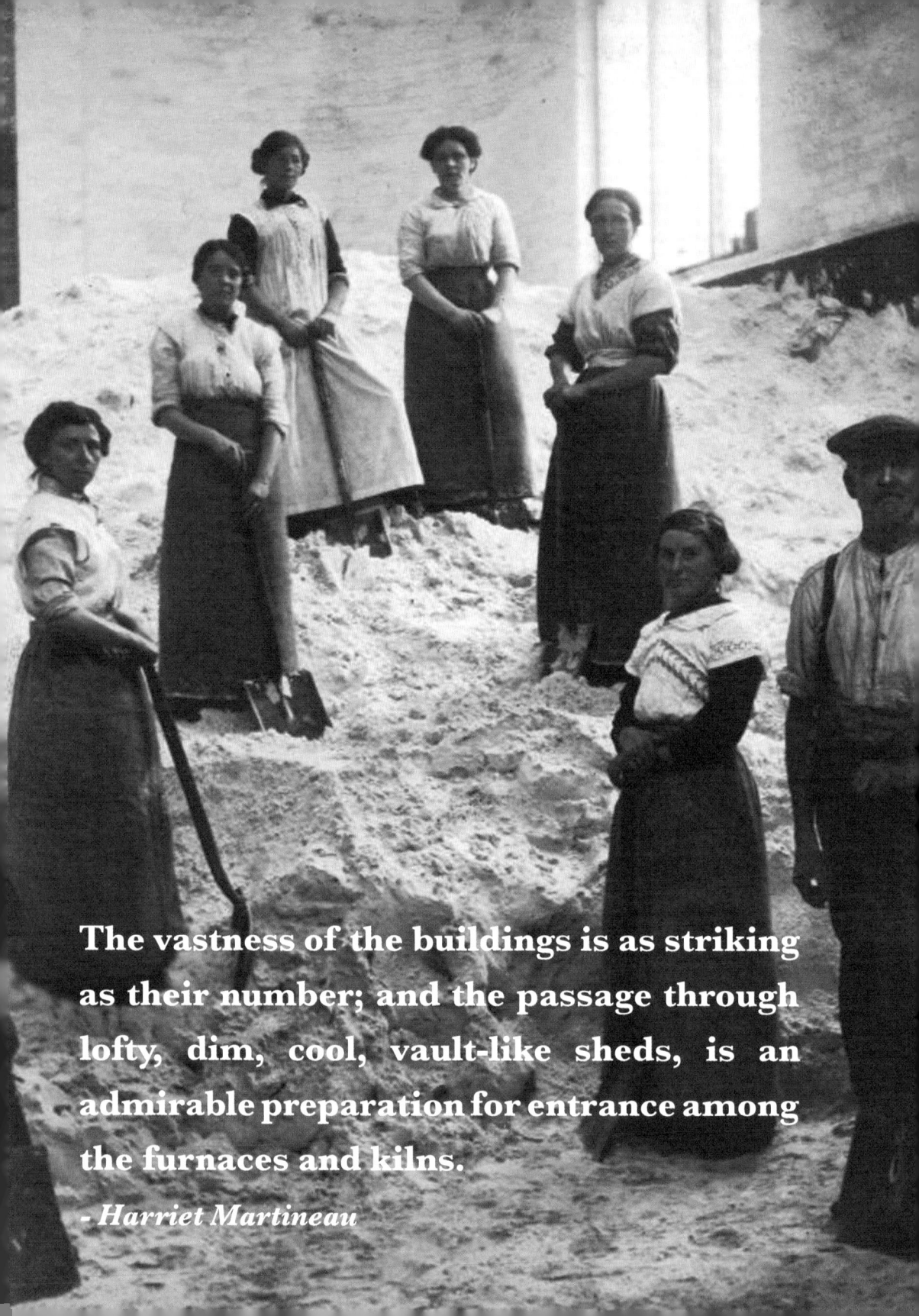

The vastness of the buildings is as striking as their number; and the passage through lofty, dim, cool, vault-like sheds, is an admirable preparation for entrance among the furnaces and kilns.

- Harriet Martineau

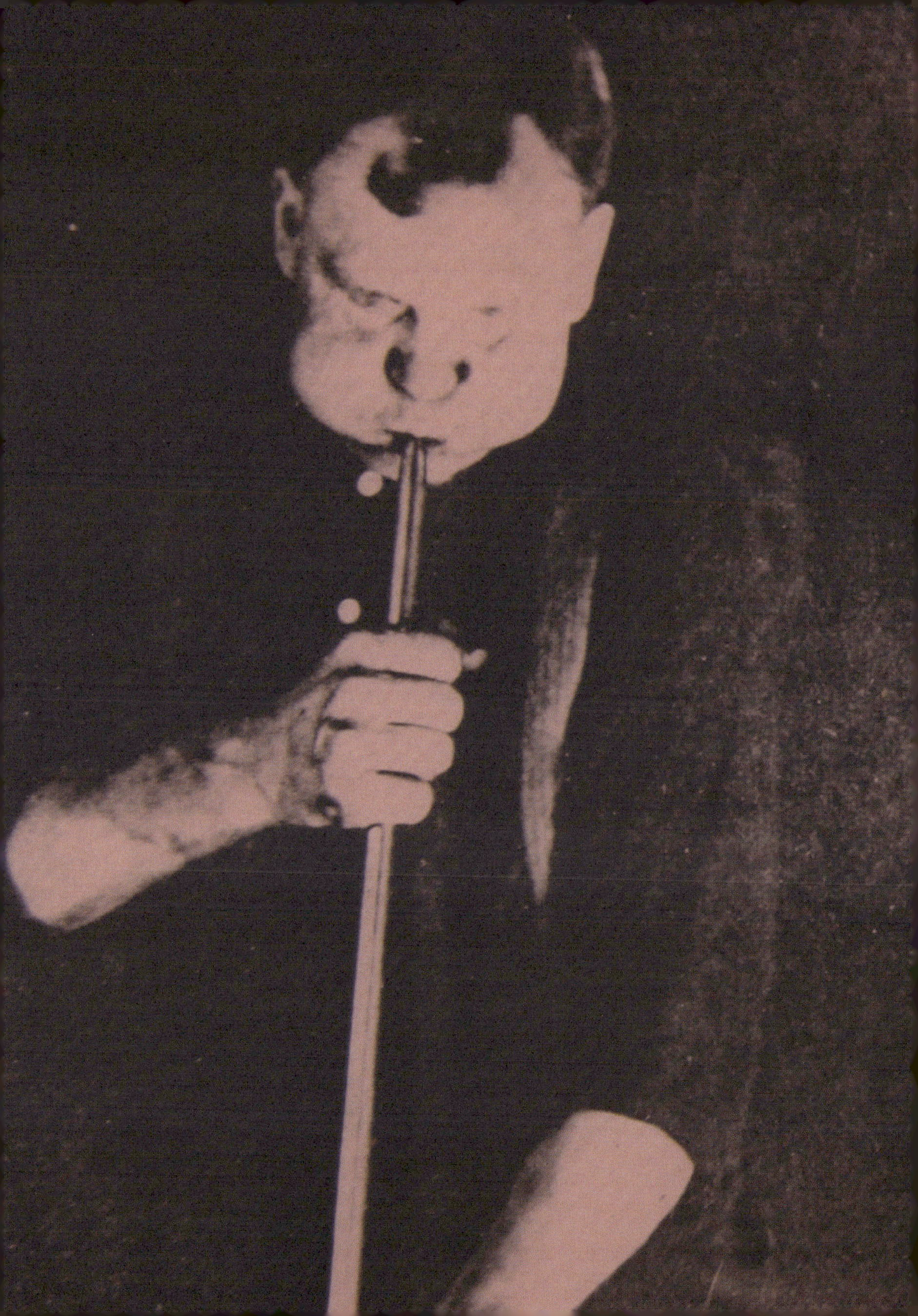

The glassworks

In 1905, Windsor Magazine, a monthly periodical, features an article on lighthouses and their 'elaborate system of signals for the guidance of mariners.' In considering 'the beautiful and interesting instruments employed in lighthouse illumination' the writer makes a visit to Chance Brothers. The writer explains that, when they showed their lenses at the Great Exhibition over 50 years ago, they 'entailed pecuniary loss, but they have gone on steadily to the present time with little or no official aid or encouragement – it is far otherwise in France, where the Government subsidises the French lighthouse builders – but with ever increasing success.' Since their first lights in 1856-57 'they have constructed over 1,000 lights of all dimensions, and they have planted them on the shores of every sea.'

Chance Brothers are now pre-eminent in their field. Apart from fine window glass, they produce the optics essential for lighthouses and all the associated mechanical equipment, the frames for the lenses, the turntables and rotating machinery, the lanterns and metalwork. Their Optical Department also produces glass for telescopes, binoculars, gun-sights, spectacle lenses and microscopes. It is true that at first, as they perfected their skills, for many years their lighthouse department ran at a considerble loss.

Their works are to be found in West Smethwick, at the boundary of Staffordshire and Worcestershire, some five miles from Birmingham, less than two from West Bromwich. On the northern side of the site, the Old Birmingham Canal separates them from iron and steel foundries. At the top end of Spon Lane, the original main gate is next to the seven-storey building (which has a cupola atop, holding a bell). Spon Lane runs north to south on the eastern side of the works, down to the Oldbury Road. (To service thirsty workers, there are over 20 pubs along Spon Lane alone.) Within 100 yards, a bridge crosses the new Birmingham canal, and alongside we find the station of the London and North-Western railway, with a branch line into the factory works. (Both canal and railway run straight as arrow in a deep cutting through the centre of the site.) Immediately we find a second works entrance, just before a line of buildings which housed the Chance schools, first set up in 1845 and now leased to the local school board. There are houses, shops and public houses opposite.

A third entrance, the one nearest the lighthouse engineering buildings, is on Oldbury Road, which marks their southern boundary. A tramline runs along here, a depot nearby, the line of houses on the corner of Spon Lane and this road once occupied by French and Belgian glassworkers. On the western boundary are the farm buildings of Blakeley Hall and its disused colliery, land that will later function as a recreation ground for Chance employees. Beyond this the canal loops down from north to southwest. The site of the works is vast, nearly 40 acres.

On the northern part of the site, almost an island contained by the two canals, was an existing crown glass works that Robert Lucas Chance purchased in 1822, expanding with a second and third glasshouse within a few years, soon recruiting the expertise of those French and Belgians to develop sheet glass. His brothers William and George also invested in the business, thus it became Chance Brothers and Company in 1832. By 1850, their growing expertise and ambition led them to develop optical apparatus for lighthouses, utilising further French know-how alongside the engineering brilliance of William's son, James Timmins Chance. They also, famously, produce the glass (950,000 square feet of rolled plate) for the 1851 Great Exhibition – the Crystal Palace – where they proudly exhibit a First Order lens to millions of visitors. This type of lens, the biggest and most powerful, is designed for use in sea and coastal lights, developed from the designs of Augustus Fresnel (1788-1827). Lower order lenses (second through to sixth) are used for smaller towers, and in channels and harbours.

Their first lighthouse commission is in 1856, for Rathlin Island off the coast of County Antrim, Northern Ireland. The second lighthouse associated with Chances also dates from this year. *The Story of Our Lighthouses and Lightships* by W.H. Davenport Adams (1891) meticulously records the details: 'Bardsey Island, lat. 52 45'. Height, 102 feet. Shows a white light for twenty-seven seconds; eclipsed for three. A fog-siren is stationed here. Cost, with buildings, £5,470 12s 6d; lantern, £2,950 16s 7d.' The island, off the Llŷn Peninsula, North Wales, was originally a haven for persecuted Christians; the lighthouse here guides ships passing through St George's Channel and the Irish Sea. The third is on the south point of Inisheer Island, one of the chain of the Aran Islands; 'a fixed white light (with a small red sector over the Finis Rock) in one of Mr. Halpin's lofty and graceful edifices, a tower of limestone measuring one hundred and twelve feet from base to vane, dating from 1857. Cost £14,252 2s 4d.'

A visit to the works is memorable: in 1852, journalist Harriet Martineau remarks: 'Visitors to the works may pass hither and thither for four or five hours together without entering the same place twice... The vastness of the buildings is as striking as their number; and the passage through lofty, dim, cool, vault-like sheds, is an admirable preparation for entrance among the furnaces and kilns.' In 1868, American consul Elihu Burritt compares it, in the moonlight, to 'a great nest of cathedrals and Turkish Mosques.' In 1872 a Japanese delegation arrives, among their number the former Prime Minister of that country. In 1878, a delegation comes from Imperial China 'in full native dress'; Margaret Chance records that there was an eclipse of the moon that evening and their guests were alarmed – 'we had to sound the gong, ring bells and beat on metal trays to frighten away evil spirits.'

Between 1855 and 1914, Chances supply a multitude of lights – 205 of the First Order, 120 of the Second, 197 of the Third, 520 of the Fourth, and 11 hyper-radial lights, all enabling the trade in goods and the movement of people, east and west. Their lights are sent to Australia, the West Indies, China, Japan, India, Mexico, Peru, Ceylon, Canada, Africa, the Crimea. A Chance lens even sits atop one of the best-known lighthouse in the United States, Heceta Head, Oregon – though historically the Yanks prefer to buy from their French competitors.

In Smethwick they build hundreds of cast iron towers and buoys, they supply light ships and produce hundreds of fog signals using whistles, bells, explosive signals, reed horns and sirens. They make the lights for the immense sea towers at the Eddystone and Bishop Rock. They improve on the design of the Incandescent Oil Vapor (I.O.V.) lamp that had been invented in France in 1898. In their works they make, cast and polish the glass, they make the lamps and burners, they erect their lighthouses in the yard and assemble their lenses in their metal frames to test, then dissemble it all, put it into boxes and ship it across the world for Chance workers to construct on site. Then to ensure the accuracy of the light in situ, a boat is sent out which checks the angle and reflection of the beam at the distances of 5 miles, 15 miles and 20 miles.

Nothing is really kept in stock as the lights are bespoke; their design depends on how tall the tower will be, what its position is to the sea, in exactly which direction the light will need to shine. Indeed, there's a great deal of science and mathematics involved and well as patient manual labour. You will find many women working here, smoothing the lighthouse glass by hand with fine emery board, carefully polishing it to a jewel-like finish.

At the turn of the century the glassworks employ some 1,800 people, across generations. The works has a lending library with some 10,000 books, a Provident Society Scheme (the 'Sick Club' as it is called), which has wide coverage in the event of sickness or death (and set up well before any legislative requirements). They have their own works doctor and within a few years Chances will also set up a technical school for higher education opportunities. No wonder people see work at Chances as both a skilled vocation and a job for life.

As one young boy arrives at the works gate on an August morning, he asks where he might find Dr Rosenhain, who has offered him the position of Analytical Chemist. Old Johnson the Gatekeeper asks his name. 'Martin,' he duly replies. 'Tom, Dick or Harry?' the gatekeeper roars back. (It's Harold actually.) He is taken to the laboratory by what seems a very circuitous route, past the rightly famed Optical Department, past a Carpenter's Shop, and then through an underground passage. The factory is hive of activity, a maze. He is told the laboratory is a very new venture and he soon finds everything pertaining to it and its denizens is viewed with suspicion by the management. They are discussing the quality and relative costs of bringing the finest sands from Leighton Buzzard or Aylesbury and the minutiae of logistics of transport by canal.

He observes the manufacture of sheet glass, rolled plate (much of which is bound for South America), coloured and spectacle glass made in pot furnaces. He finds the furnaces dark and dirty places, the glass spooned out of the tanks with huge ladles and big strong men to blow it. He finds it remarkable that the cylinders of sheet glass are blown without the aid of any machine. He can see these huge fellows swinging the unfinished cylinder round and round to elongate it. They have cheeks like balloons. When he first sees optical glass being made, it is in pots in a coal-fired furnace at the base of a cone shaped chimney stack. Tunnels beneath the furnace help draw air in, mix it with gas and pre-heat it, allowing the furnace to operate at higher temperatures. The factory even has its own gas works on site. Martin settles into the hustle and bustle. He will work at Chances until his retirement in the 1950s, all the time marvelling at their technical achievements.

In this same year the new lighthouse at Portland Bill rises up, Chances make lights of varying sizes, along with lanterns and towers for locations all over the map. Holy Island and Butt of Lewis, Scotland; Tasman Island, Tasmania; One Fathom Point, Straits Settlement; Greca Point, Natal; Martin River, Canada; Port Sudan, Egypt; Isla Queriquina and Punta Felix, Chile; Nicholski Island and Cape Young, Korea; Double Island, Newfoundland; Prospect Harbour, United States; as well as Fiji and Argentina. Far, far away from Smethwick.

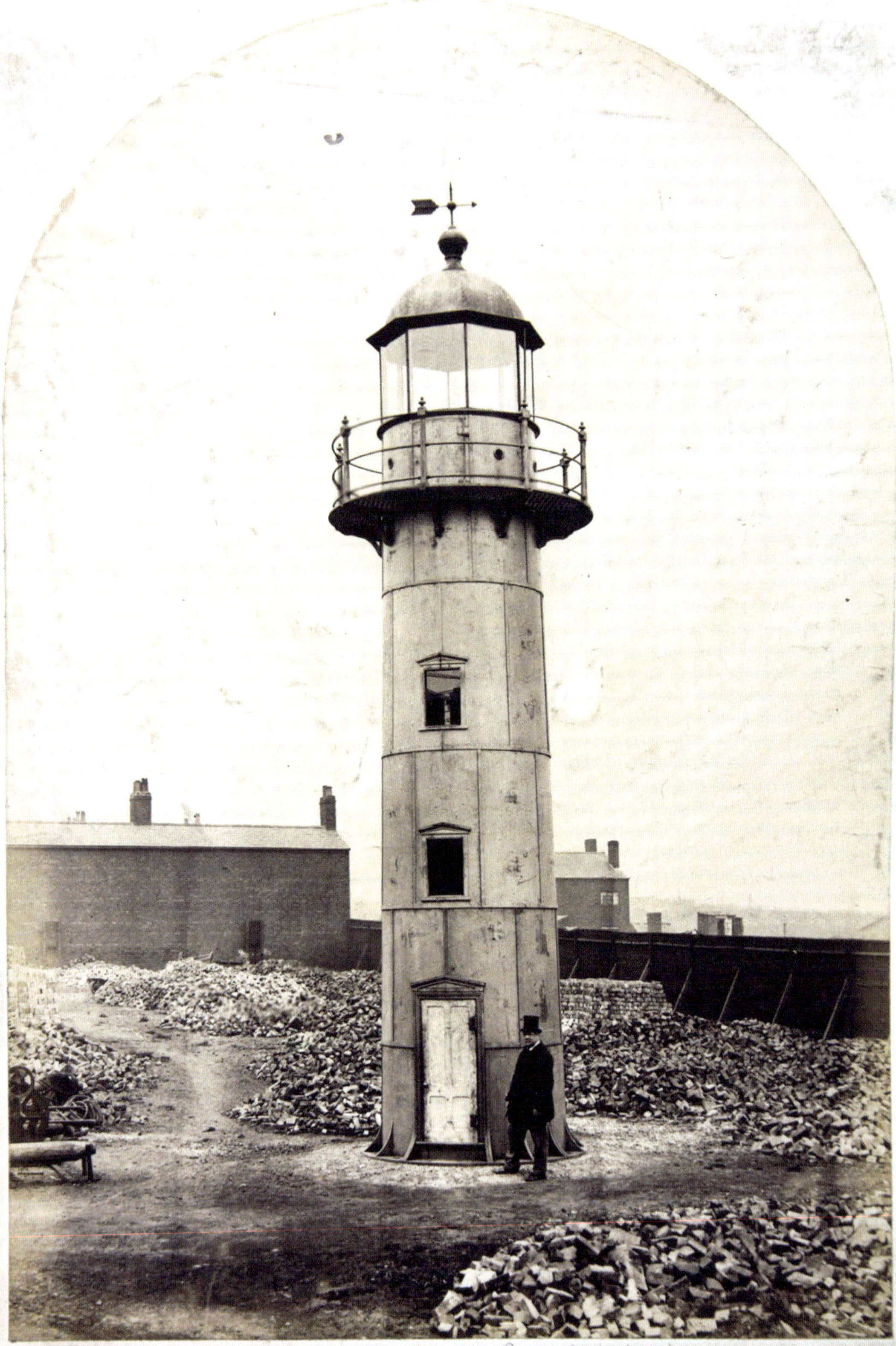

W. A. Perry. Chief draughtsman

Top Portion of Cast Iron Tower, with Lantern
of 2,150 Metres diameter inside glazing, for
Punta Coles Lighthouse, Peru.

CONSTRUCTED BY
CHANCE BROTHERS AND CO., LIMITED
Lighthouse Works,
SMETHWICK, BIRMINGHAM, ENGLAND
1919

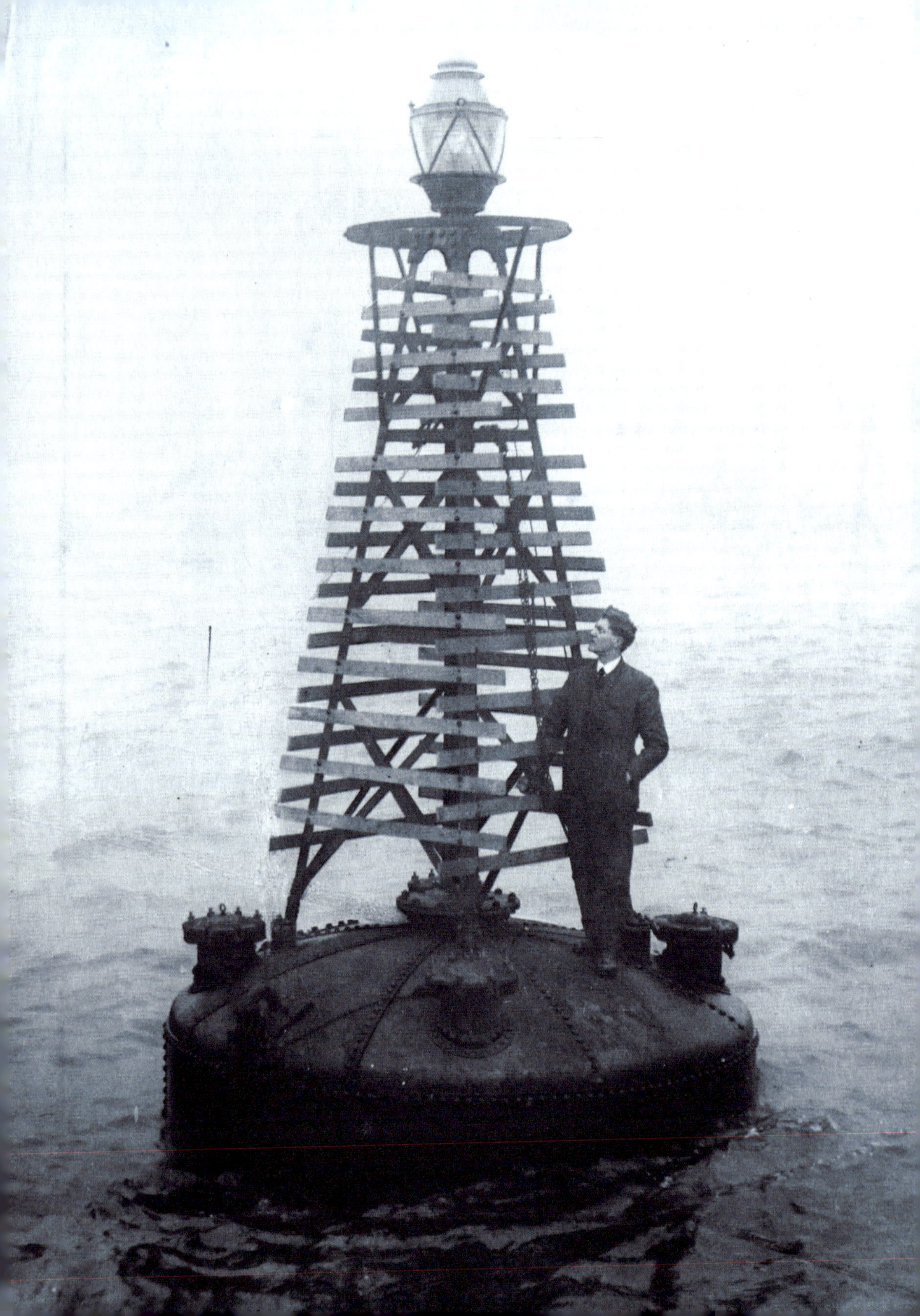

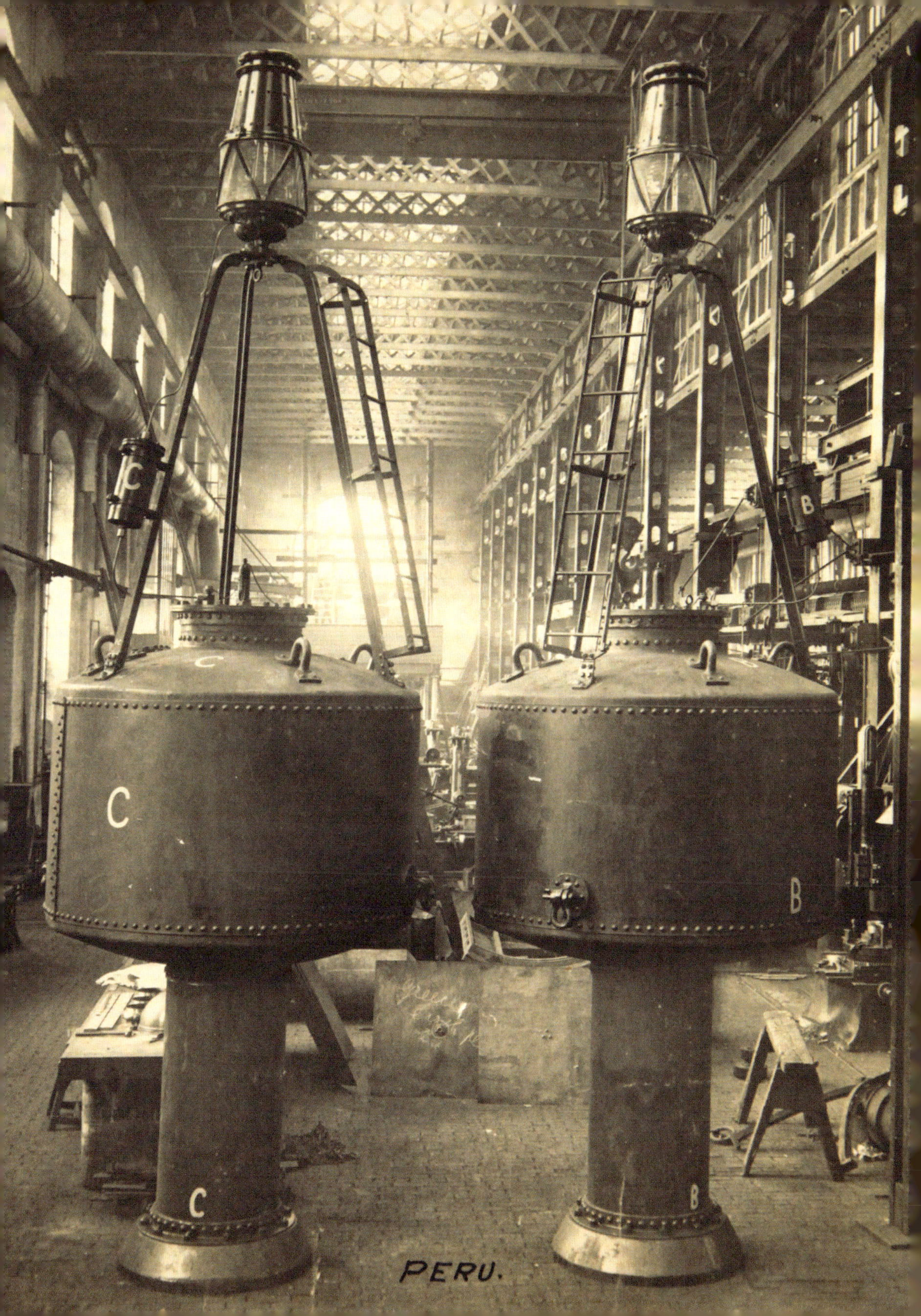
C
C
C
B
B
B
PERU.

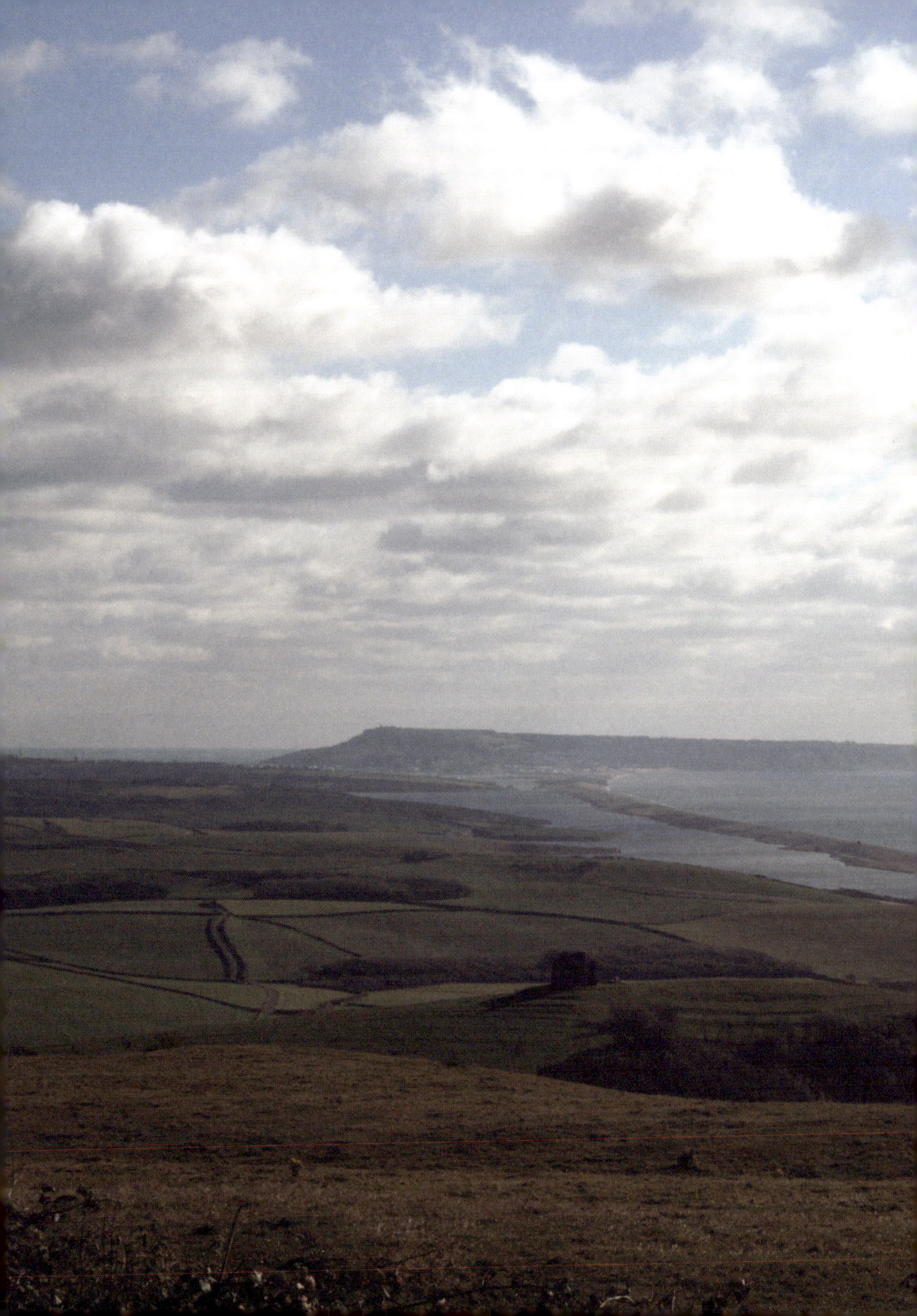

The road from Wyke Regis to Portland is by the attenuated ridge of the Chesil Beach which connects the so-called island to the mainland. The road is some two miles in length, and for monotony and tediousness it cannot be surpassed. To a tired pedestrian on a summer's day the glaring penitential path is little less than torture. The road appears to have the power of extending itself without end, like a treadmill placed horizontally. The place has no variableness nor shadow of turning. It is ever pebbles, pebbles, pebbles. The only relief are the telegraph poles which border this road of the Wandering Jew, and which furnish the blessed diversion of something to count.

- *Sir Frederick Treves, Highways and Byways in Dorset, 1906*

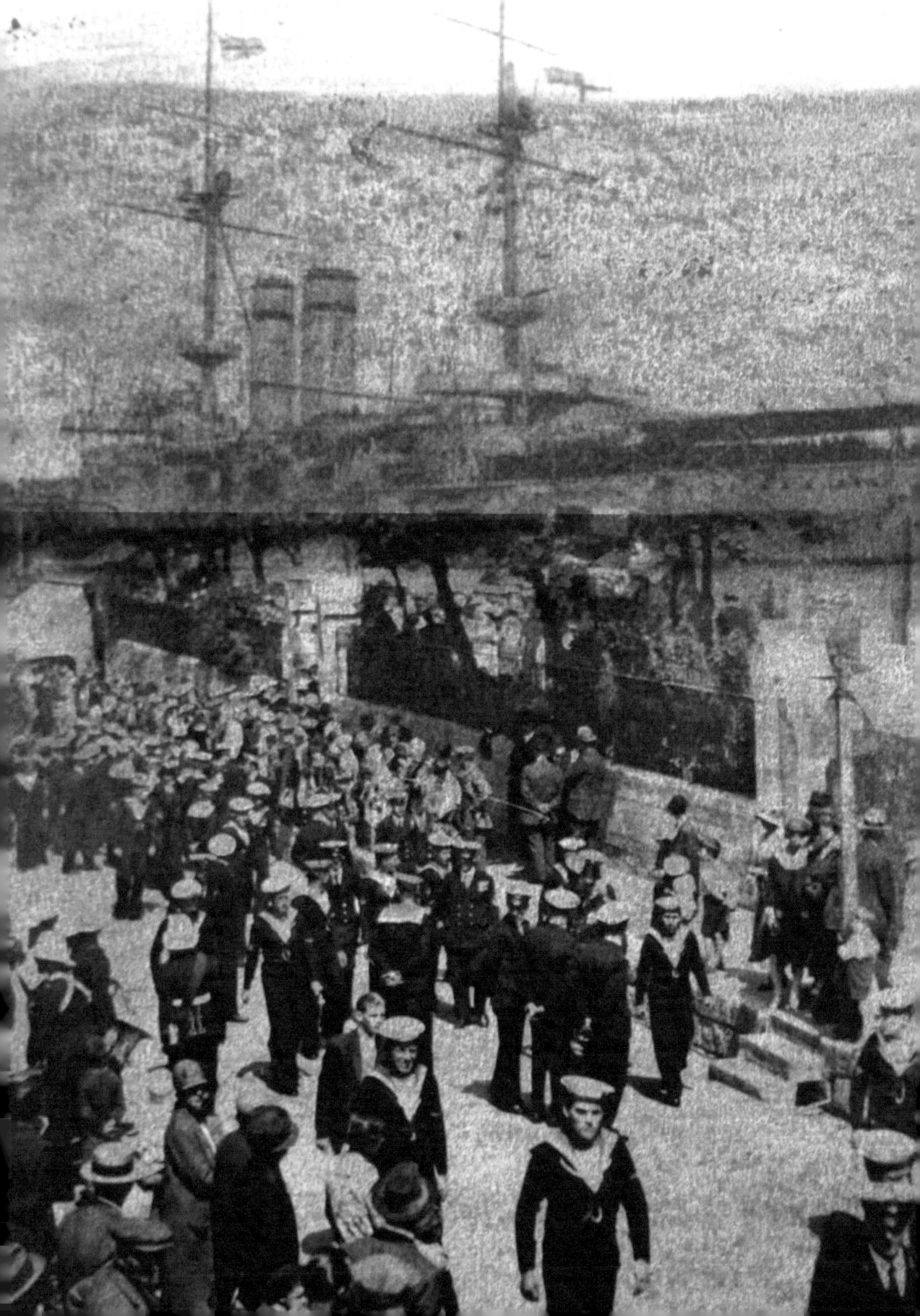

In the Navy you can sail the seven seas

At the beginning of the 20th century, Britain controls one third of the world's population, her Empire now the largest in the world with an estimated 345 million people. Her naval and merchant fleets are found in every port on six continents. The building of Portland harbour, breakwater and fortifications, one of the supreme engineering constructions of the Victorian era, has created the biggest deepwater port in Europe. What was once a 'harbour of refuge' now functions primarily to service the Royal Navy. The waters of Portland Roads are enclosed by two huge breakwater arms, each with two sections, the northern arm only recently completed – at its end stands a brand new revolving light on top of an iron tower, both made by Chance Brothers, which guides vessels through the main entrance. These breakwaters are pierced by three openings, of sufficient width to admit a battleship and capable of being closed by heavy booms.

All is not well within the ranks – during the recent South African War there was an increase in soldiers' pay but none for sailors. Lower deck pay has remained almost unchanged in 50 years, and living conditions on board are archaic. Sleeping quarters are crowded. Most of the crew has to make do with a wooden mess tub for a bath, which is also used for washing up utensils. Sailors purchase and maintain their own uniform as well as subsidise their basic rations. Victualling is a major cause of complaint. The standard ration allows each man one cooked meal a day – $1\,^{1}/_{4}$ lbs of biscuit or $1\,^{1}/_{2}$ lbs of soft bread, together with 1 lb of fresh meat and 1 lb of fresh vegetables. When fresh items are unavailable, 1 lb of salt pork and $^{1}/_{2}$ pound of split peas are issued every other day, or salted beef with flour, suet, raisins.

There are arguments higher up about the role of the post-Victorian Navy, calls for more reforms and modernisation. In 1905 the Earl of Seaborne, First Lord of the Admiralty, states to Parliament: 'To maintain the daily employment, the wages, the food of the population – that is the function of the Navy. It is not only to guard your shores and those of every colony and dependency in the Empire, but it is to bring the bread to the working men of this country, to bring to the loom, to the forges, to the factories, the means by which they can earn the wages to support wife and children. That, and nothing less, is the duty of the Navy.' Though others feel the duty of the Navy is not to defend anything, but rather to attack the fleets of the enemy wherever they may be. They are worrying less about the French now that the recent Entente Cordiale has resolved their disputes over colonies. As for the Russians, they've gone and shot themselves in the foot. It's the intentions of Germany that are now being studied carefully. They say, Germany stands where we once stood, on the threshold of the future.

Though the system is slowly being restructured, a young fellow still might have mixed feelings about a career in the Royal Navy. With the mighty Dreadnought under construction (built and launched in less than a year), they plan to scrap over 150 old vessels. Two years ago, only half the Fleet had a wireless set; now the Admiralty can send orders to ships anywhere within home waters and the Mediterranean. Trials have been undertaken at Portland Bill with Marconi sets; there is now a building for this purpose near to the old Higher Lighthouse. (Before long they will be the first to make direct radio contact with Gibraltar). All officer cadets now receive common training up to Lieutenant's exams. Engineers are getting more advanced technical training, becoming gunnery, torpedo or navigation specialists. With steamships, an officer needs intimate knowledge of the workings of the ship, of all the machinery, guns, torpedoes and electric lights, far more than simply control of the motive power. Birching in public for boy recruits is about to be abolished, to be replaced by private caning (and that only after a formal hearing), though Vice Admiral Penrose writes to The Times to complain: 'British youths have been birched and caned from time immemorial and yet the race has not turned out badly as a whole.'

A fresh-faced Sub-Lieutenant is posted for 12 months to the Channel Fleet at Portland. He has served with the Mercantile Marine, traditionally a vital source of manpower for the Navy but less so these days, as nearly a half of its sailors are not even British. He finds himself aboard a battleship, originally intended for service in Asia. Commissioned 6 years earlier, with a crew of over 700 officers and ratings, the ship is smaller and lighter than predecessors. Torpedoes will later sink her during the Dardanelles Campaign in 1915, but now she resides in Portland Roads. 'Portland is the very best port in the world,' argues Admiral Lord Beresford. 'There is no other place where you can keep your men ready like Portland.'

On watch duty, our Sub-Lieutenant might well agree. As he scans his surroundings in the mellow light of a late afternoon, what a marvellous panorama to behold! The rampart of Chesil Beach to the west, the little stone and slate houses of Chiswell at the foot of the Isle, the rugged cliffs at East Weares and tipped spoil from the quarries, the single steep road that leads from Fortune's Well to the top. The island is an immense solid block of limestone, just over 4 miles long and 1½ miles wide. It rises sharply on the landward side to 500 feet then slopes away to the Bill. He looks up at the Verne Citadel, an enormous fortress above the dockyard. To build it they sliced the top off the hill like a boiled egg. Stone dug out from the defensive ditches (120 feet wide and 70 feet deep in places) went into the construction of the outer breakwater – some 1,500,000 tons of it, thanks to convict labour. Almost as soon as it was finished the fort was out of date, its big guns powerless against the new weapons of the war – those torpedoes, mines and submarines, not to mention the coming airplane – and most are removed by 1906. Instead, he is told, there are 12 pounder quick firing guns and Maxims sited across each harbour mouth, with larger guns at the pier heads. Batteries at East Weares, Blacknor and Upton are equipped with 9.2 inch and 6 inch guns. Others are mounted the circular Breakwater Fort. Near to him, he can see the coaling pier, newly rebuilt, and destroyer berths alongside bustling Castletown, where the cooks and stewards of the Fleet keep the public houses busy. He sees the Tudor castle by the waterside (now used for officer accommodation), the naval hospital, new oil tanks under construction and a line of rails down a steep incline, this a gravity powered tramway by which they move quarried stone from Tophill to the boats waiting below. If he turns to look inland, beyond the cargo lighters scurrying between ships, past the despoiled ruin of Sandsfoot castle, then he will spy the pier of Whitehead torpedo factory extending into the water – something Herr Tirpitz would no doubt take great interest in – then Ferry Bridge and the rail line that runs along the causeway back to Victoria Square at Chiswell, at the foot of the Isle.

Well protected indeed, Portland Roads is crowded with ships of the Fleet, some recalled from China Station. From a distance they look magnificent. Not as colourful as they once were, these ships are now painted in that shade called 'battleship grey' – though the torpedo boats and torpedo boat destroyers are painted black. The old training ships have been moved to make space in the water and there is little enough room for merchants now. The colour of the Fleet is also the colour of the Isle; from his vantage point aship, he may try in vain to spot some trees. A local author has likened it, not unkindly, to 'a jagged browed Sphinx.'

At first, the Sub-Lieutenant does not find his new appointment at all welcoming. When he goes down to the gunroom, he finds it unbearably stuffy, full of tobacco smoke. There's three young chaps playing cards, no more than 20 (the average age of a naval rating is 21) who ask him if he's brought his chest, as there's nowhere to put clothes. Fortunately, he does have his things packed in some boxes. As an engineer, a suit of canvas overalls when crawling in tight corners is recommended; the Admiralty issues 12 yards of coarse duck for use by each engineer every year for the making of overall suits. They also say, 'A white cashmere neck wrap may be useful to put on if duty calls you on deck.' Socks should be of the strongest material, as it is difficult to get them darned at sea. As for private clothes, he has a blue sage suit and a Norfolk jacket for a ramble on shore, with an overcoat for the evening when the weather turns chill. There may be a space found for a cricket bag or for a rod and gun, or maybe not. He knows that only essential books should be taken aboard; they have to resist rough treatment from cockroaches and occasionally from seawater. (Castor oil is recommended to protect bindings from insects.) Finally, it is essential to pack a pocket book, in order to note defects on his rounds.

His gunroom companions ask him if he'd like a drink; he notes there seems to be a lot of drinking going on. On this occasion he declines, as he is more concerned with where he might sleep. He wanders around the ship until a senior engineering fellow gets a man to finally sling him a hammock back in the gunroom. The following morning, when he goes to the bathroom he finds it ankle deep in water; no proper bathing facilities in his opinion. He puts on his frock coat and goes on deck for inspection. At 10.30 am there is a mass on deck, with no sermon. The paymaster plays some hymns on a harmonium. For an officer, at 8.00 am there is porridge and fish eggs for breakfast, for lunch at 12.00 a heated up dish of non-description is served, with some cold meat slices and cheese; dinner at 7.30 pm offers him soup, fish, entrée, joint, cheese, followed by coffee. His mess bills for one month are £2 and 12s, though you have to pay extra for dessert and afternoon tea. The food is passable, nowhere near as bad as on the now infamous Potemkin. He is bothered that there are only two domestics to serve a mess of 20, the tables are not decorated and the cutlery could do with a good clean. When he finally speaks to the Captain and explains he was expecting somewhat better accommodation, a cabin perhaps, the Captain is dismissive of the thought. You're in the Navy now, lad. Our Sub-Lieutenant cheers up once he secures the services of a marine to act as his servant.

Rather like the life of a lighthouse keeper, as novelty wears off, routine takes its place. He settles into it. He has various drills to attend to; general quarters, fire quarters, collision quarters, man and arm ship. There are inspections of the men, in order that any irregularity in dress may not catch the attention of the Captain, who does a weekly round on Sunday. He has to check through equipment, that fire engines are ready for action, that steam pressures, feed pumps, boiler gauge glasses, ventilating fans are all in good order, that bearings are running cool. There's coaling to be done to prepare the engines, ready for manoeuvres out at sea. That's hard work and not something the crew look forward to – though the Admiralty are now testing the viability of oil as fuel.

He is on deck to supervise the bathing of ratings, who clean themselves in the sea; a boat is lowered and lifelines are kept handy to avoid any accidents – on a nearby ship recently, a stoker was knocked overboard and killed. Then, so many tattoos are revealed to the viewer: a fully rigged ship across a broad back, rings on the second and third fingers of a left hand, a heart and cross on a left forearm, a pierced heart, true love and clasped hands on a right forearm, a five pointed compass star on a bicep, anchors, dragons, a dagger through a rose, swallows to find your way home, mermaids, names or initials. He goes on watch three times a day. Post arrives twice a day. The afternoons in port are generally quiet and offer a little time for light reading below decks. The Prince of Storytellers, G. A. Henty, the celebrated author of many a stirring adventure, is mourned. He passed away not so long ago, aboard his yacht in Weymouth; the last book published, *Conduct and Courage*, tells a young man who battles with the French and pirates in the Napoleonic Wars. If Henty is not quite your cup of tea, then *The Sea Wolf* by Jack London and *Nostromo* by Joseph Conrad are popular maritime novels of the day. There's many a patriotic fellow attracted to the service by such romantic adventures, the lure of the sea, that and unemployment.

He may peruse the local newspapers. Miss Dorothy White is offering lessons in Dancing and Calisthenics, Skipping, Ball Exercises and Fancy Dancing in Dorchester and Weymouth. The Orient Company's Steamships offer Pleasure Cruises to Sunny Lands. A 41-day trip to Greece, Turkey, Asia Minor, Egypt and Malta aboard the SS. Ormuz (once called the fastest ship in the world) will cost 35 guineas and upwards. An inscription above the entrance to their First Class Saloon reads: 'Were the World a Ring of Gold, Ormuz would be its Diamond.' A 17-day trip to Spain, Gibraltar, Portugal aboard SS. Ophir costs 15 guineas upwards. What wonders are now within reach for the common man!

In a series of notices, Dorset County Council announces the intention of the police to prosecute any person who kills or takes any of the following wild birds: Bittern, Buzzard, Chough, Crossbill, Goldfinch, Great Crested Grebe, Hen and Marsh Harrier, Hobby, Hoopoe, Kingfisher, Nightjar,

Golden Oriole, Osprey, various Owls, Raven, Spoonbill, Bearded Tit, Woodpeckers, Woodlarks. There is another extensive list of some 90 birds not to be shot, trapped or ensnared, eggs not to be taken. Cormorant and Shag are exceptions to this ruling.

There's a prominent advertisement promoting emigration to Western Australia: 100 Acres Free! Splendid Climate! Assisted passages from £9. For particulars apply to Western Australian Government, 15 Victoria Street, London. Another makes his stomach rumble: 'A real Irish stew, my dear, will repay you the care you take with it,' says Dame Goodsoul. 'Get two pounds of mutton pieces, the same quantity of potatoes, a half pound of onions and a Penny Packet of Edwards Desiccated Soup – E-D-S gives that stew a flavour and a taste that will do your heart good.' The mess stew is acceptable, but oh for a plate of some good home cooking. If any meal causes Biliousness or Indigestion then Carters Little Liver Pills might solve any such problem, available in all good chemists: also recommended for Sick Headache, Torpid Liver, Constipation, Sallow Skin, Dizziness, or Furred Tongue. Small Dose, Small Price. Sugar coated and purely vegetable. A copy of the Portland Telegram indicates where to go ashore should he have the need – perhaps F. L. Simmonds, lowest store prices, cash only.

Simmonds dispenses prescriptions with 'Accuracy the first consideration,' and assures his clientele 'No unqualified assistance employed.' He also supplies photographic materials, a now fashionable pastime. W. J. Comben, tailor and outfitter, promises his indigo blue serge suits will retain their colour. H. Gill, the Army and Navy Boot and Shoe Maker, can also provide oilcloths and leggings; some good business to be had there no doubt.

In Wakeham, local gossip – the body of a woman is found in a large iron tank at the back of some houses. She is reported 'quite dead.' They say she had been rather strange in her mind for some time past and had told the milkman that when he next called with the morning milk it would be the last time he would serve her. She could neither read nor write and had taken some pictures from her bedroom and laid them next to the tank, with the apparent intention of drawing attention to it. The inquest simply gives a verdict of 'Found drowned.'

In the afternoons, day-trippers, who arrive on steamers from across Weymouth bay, visit ships in harbour; often they are allowed aboard. There's many a young rating who then takes the same steamer to go ashore, only be fleeced by the Crown and Anchor dice schools aboard them. An officer has to be seen to keep his wits about him – when he takes shore leave, he will visit Weymouth and thereabouts by train, occasionally entertaining friends down from London with tea at the old Gloucester Lodge (replete with comfort, electric light throughout) on the Esplanade, followed by a stroll through Alexandra Gardens to the bandstand. There are daily concerts in the season, and many a regimental or naval band practicing a patriotic tune. It has to be admitted there is not much of interest in the town for an antiquarian; only popular amusements, bath chairs, donkeys and goat-chaises, cocoa nut shys and shooting galleries frequented by blue-jerseyed loafers. A trip to the interior of Portland offers another possibility – a 'most interesting all day excursion' – though the visitor who is no hill climber is advised to go by train to Easton, where they will find a well-appointed new public garden, making this their starting point. The branch line is a great convenience, the GWR train passing the dockyard and rising along the eastern cliff edge, through deep cuttings in the rock to the terminus there. They may find Mr Dixon, resplendent in white, plying his trade, selling ice cream from his horse and cart. They may decide to stretch their legs with a few hours walk back, enjoying the splendid views and fresh air. The streets are white with dust from the quarries, the main (and rightly famed) occupation of the Isle. Indeed, they say Portland is the Mother of London.

On a clear day, on these perambulations, you might see as far as the Isle of Wight, but there is no road yet down to the new lighthouse at the Bill. It is still rugged terrain. Even Sir Frederick Treves, the famous surgeon who cycles 2,000 miles around the County to compile his newly published popular travelogue *Highways and Byways of Dorset*, does not venture further than Church Ope Cove, which he finds 'a genial nook.' As for the rest of this 'sour island,' overall he decides it is a melancholy place. He describes the quarries as though he has just put down a copy of *War of the Worlds*. The cranes 'wave titanic arms against the sky, which might be the tentacles of some leviathan insect, or weave threads of wire over the abyss like the strands of some unearthly spiders-web; smoke rises from gasping engines, while now and then a block of stone glides hissing across the void like a fearsome bird. All round are heaps of litter, piles of wind-blown dust, patches of scarred earth, and deserted pits which are becoming covered with a green mould. To intensify the allurement of this curious scene, the air is made to tremble now and then by the firing of a gun in the fort or in the harbour, the boom of which is re-echoed sulkily from the sea cliff.'

Treves also reports on the convict teas arranged for tourists, which are timed to give views of the prisoners as they leave for work in the evening. This has been a pastime for some decades now. As far back as 1874, Mr T. G. Green of The Eagle Tavern was advertising: 'The Place to see the Convicts. Tea, Coffee and Refreshments provided at Moderate Charges. Chops and Steaks at the Shortest Notice. Good Accommodation for the Visitors. Choice Wines and Spirits. Prime Dorset Ales in the Finest Condition. Feed for Horse, &c, at Moderate Prices.' Treves considers this 'a morbid diversion,' as he muses on the plight of those incarcerated, who on a summer's day must look down on the excursionists arriving, those families picnicking on the beach, happy couples rowing in the bay. 'At night,' he concludes, 'in their solitary cells these sounds and sights must burn into their very souls.'

Visiting a few years earlier with her father, Beatrix Potter writes, 'Portland is a curiosity to see once. A mixture of Gibraltar and one's notion of the Holy Land. Very like Gibraltar only flat-topped...' The sight of convicts working in this 'stony wilderness' did not particularly appeal to her either. Due to the prison population, as well as the military and naval presence, Portland's population has tripled in just a few years; it now stands at 15,199. Strangers, those known locally as 'Kimberlins,' will surely soon outnumber the natives. To Treves, this place 'has no more pretence to charm than has the barrel of a dismounted cannon.'

Our Navy fellows and their acquaintances may take a more charitable view as they consult their Red Guide – which tells them the atmosphere 'has a briny and Neptunian savour, and is redolent of the ocean.' As for the jailbirds themselves being escorted from the gate to the quarry: 'Though in the worst of taste, it is unfortunately often considered quite *en regie* for visitors to watch the procession of convicts to and from their work.' There are several picture postcards to attest to this. W. T. Wallis at The Library, Easton, has the largest stock of views, both black & white and coloured – 'all the latest novelties...' He also carries Bibles and Hymn books, newspapers and magazines. W. A. Attwooll, who supplies groceries, medicines and coal at his various establishments, is a keen photographer himself and documents much of the island, some of which he turns into pictorial postcards for sale, a lucrative business now that the Post Office have relaxed their rules and allow pictures to appear on the front and messages with the address to appear on the back. He recently presented a photograph of the old Easton town pump to the Town Council, a reminder of the recent times when the Isle relied entirely on water from wells – some still do, as not all are convinced of the idea of receiving water from a tap.

Our sightseers are reliably informed that at the Grove nearby, St Peters Church has an interesting mosaic of the Four Evangelists made by one of the convicts, Constance Kent. Aged 16 in 1860, she had been arrested for the murder of her baby step-brother. She was not tried and only prosecuted 5 years later, then having made confession – though there were doubts as to its veracity. Released in 1885, she emigrated to Australia. St Peters had been built in 1870, with an abundance of prison labour of course, the pulpit and lectern carved from Portland stone by 'Irish Fenians and Whitechapel thieves.' Thank the Lord that even amongst the worst of us there is hope for redemption.

The windswept graveyard at St George's Church may provide them with another morbid diversion. The headstones tell their short stories. Here you will find Chief Petty Officer George John Leggett, who served on HMS Discovery Arctic Expedition of 1875-1876, died December 1909, age 57. Or Benjamin Scriven, who was accidentally shot by the Steward in the East India Dock London in October 1875, aged 24 years. One inscription reads: 'SACRED To the Memory of WILLIAM PEARCE, Who was killed by Lightning, While on duty in Her Majestie's service, On Portland Beach November 29th 1858, Leaving a widow and five children, To lament his loss, Aged 33 Years.'

Convicts Proceeding to Work

Portland Bill and New Lighthouse

One grave holds Carpenter Jamieson of the ship Avalanche, and 'five other names unknown who were drownde in attempting to land in Chesil Cove on the morning September 12th 1877' – this was after the collision of 2 ships the previous night when 106 lives were lost. Here you will also find the grave of Mary Way, shot in the back by members of a Naval Press Gang, who opened fire on a crowd of protestors at Easton on 2nd April 1803; 'And died of the wound the 21st of May the same Year' age of 21. Her stone reads:

Here Immortality with beauty lies
Confin'd from Earth to kindred skies
Her Life was short her Death severe
Stop Reader, think and shed a tear

Our naval officer must return to his ship at the end of the day, his friends to their moderately priced boarding house, dog-tired by their exertions yet enlightened. Sightseeing is, as the Red Guide reminds them, not a duty but a pleasure. They may even find time to pen some lines to loved ones on the back of their selection of postcards.

Harry is looking well. A life on the ocean wave seems to suit him. Jolly company as usual. It is glorious but we have had both cold, wind and rain since we came down, but had a fair share of fine days. We may come over to see you in October but it depends on the weather. Hope you are well.
Much love, Yours, Bea

Other sailors ashore may opt for a night or two accommodation at the Wesleyan Sailors and Soldiers Home at Underhill, which has rooms for 30 men, a dining room, baths, a Temperance refreshment bar, and both a reading and recreation room. It offers comfort, clean sheets and some privacy, and it's well patronised – in just one year over 4,000 beds and 1,162 hot baths have been provided. All is well as the moon rises over the eternal sea, its stillness deceptive. Here they may dream in peace, of fish, of love, of commerce, of wrecks, of storms, of fair-weather, of good fortune.

The battleship is soon tasked with target and gunnery practice. As boilers are stoked and the steam is got up, our Sub-Lieutenant ensures pictures are removed from the walls and any moveable or breakable objects stored away. Everything on deck must be secured. Off Chesil Beach, a 20-year-old torpedo boat is used as a target. Though filled with cork to keep her afloat, she sinks pretty quickly after being hit. He goes into the foremost turret to observe the action. There are twin turrets both fore and aft, with 12-inch 35-calibre guns, with 4 men working the weapon, hardly any room to move inside, and more crew in the shell room below. Shells are loaded automatically on a tray, up they come, the breech opens and closes, a hydraulic rammer pushes the shell home and the charge is put in by hand. All this should only take 30 seconds. Then BOOM! The noise is terrific, vibrating throughout the ship and across the bay. It gives him a horrible headache. They can hear the firing right across the Isle, something local folk are getting used to. At the end of the exercises, the ships steam past the brand new lighthouse at the Bill, surely one more example of Britain's maritime expertise. Rule Britannia.

Let's go back awhile. As the builders survey the land, making ready to cut the foundations for the new light, while the order for the lens is studied in the glass factory in Smethwick and drawings amended, 45 ships from the Russian Baltic Fleet pass this way, as they journey 18,000 nautical miles from Latvia to Manchuria, shoveling 3,000 tons of coal a day. In October 1904, on a foggy night at Dogger Bank, they open fire on fishing boats from

Hull, thinking they are Japanese torpedo boats. Panic. Hysteria. There's talk again of war with Russia; British cruisers shadow the Russian fleet as it comes down the Channel, following to the Bay of Biscay and along the Portuguese coast.

29 year old Eugene Politovsky, Chief Engineer aboard the flagship Knyaz Suvorov, on his first cruise, writes to his wife: 'Passing by England this morning I saw her southern shores, which were faintly visible in the mist. Yes, there was "Foggy Albion." Involuntarily I pondered over this clod of earth – so powerful, so rich, so proud, and so ill disposed towards us. We are only three hours journey from London and six by rail from Paris. Many varieties of birds settle on the ship, tired and exhausted by their long flight. The crew feed them and let them go. I am depressed – fearfully depressed. Anxiety presses on my soul! What would I not give to be with you now! Again I have not slept all night. How tiring it all is!' In another letter he tells her: 'They are cunning, powerful at sea, and insolent everywhere. All nations hate England, but it suits them to tolerate her. If you could only hear how furiously Spaniards abuse the English! They shake their fists and nearly foam at the mouth. If they only could, they would gladly play some low trick on them. How many impediments has this "Ruler of the Seas" put on our voyage? Every impediment has come from Britannia.'

In May 1905, as the new lighthouse tower begins its ascent, the Japanese annihilate that Russian fleet at the Battle of Tsushima and Politovsky goes down with his ship. At Portland Naval base, they are astonished by this turn of events and what they may herald. Just a few weeks after the new First Order lens is lit at the Bill, the King will unveil a new kind of fighting vessel at Portsmouth, the Dreadnought, and he christens it with a bottle of Australian wine.

At this time, in the General Election, there is a landslide victory for the Liberals. The Liberals have been campaigning vigorously for months and boisterous meetings have been held on the Isle. The Wesleyan schoolroom in Fortune's Well has hosted the Liberal candidate for South Dorset, 31-year-old Thomas Scarisbrick, former Mayor of Southport. In parody of the well-known hymn, the audience sing 'Onward, Liberals, Onwards.' At the Masonic Hall, Colonel Brymer, the sitting Conservative MP, now into his 60s, an excellent shot by all accounts, is met with thunderous applause. He speaks of the vexed question of imported Chinese labour in South Africa undercutting wages, the Education Act, and the need for tariff reform, the latter supported by arguments from the stone traders. The next day he speaks at the Jubilee Hall, Easton, which is also full, despite a counter demonstration from the Radicals at the Council Schools. All speakers berate the ability of the Liberals to offer any governance whatsoever which would be of any benefit to the workingman. Yet across the country the Conservatives suffer a crushing defeat, including here, and the triumphant Scarisbrick arrives in his carriage to address the voters in Victoria Square, Chiswell. As the night darkens, the high winds and the crowd of people with repeating cheers combine to drown out his voice. Few actually hear his speech. At the Underhill Club a free and easy smoking concert is held later that evening to celebrate his victory. Mr Sansom, who has been a well-respected Chair of the local council, keeps a wary eye on the proceedings of the day; 61 years old, 'a quarryman among quarrymen,' he knows a fair bit about the affairs of the world and the Empire, having worked constructing railway stations and bridges in India. He is now the manager at the biggest quarry by far on the Isle. Many of his men, along with the local fisher folk, are in the crowds. He had supported Colonel Brymer's campaign, toasting on more than one occasion his parliamentary record, but now that's over. The gallant Colonel did not prove to be in such fine trim as they had thought.

While a prime characteristic of Portland has been insularity, the times are rapidly changing. The new government has an agenda for reform and aims to tackle the evils of poverty – they will introduce free school meals, school medical inspections, pensions, a children's charter, labour exchanges and national insurance, compensation for industrial accidents. They will introduce a Shops Act to grant shop workers a half-day a week off and limit working hours to 60. They will set the working day for miners at 8 hours. Following the debacle in South Africa, when it turned out so many Army volunteers proved physically unfit to fight, they aim to create a new generation of healthy people. Even though the policy of this new government is to reduce armaments, the increasing Naval personnel and others engaged in government work at Portland will continue to dominate the area for decades yet. The coming of the Dreadnought launches a naval arms race between Britain and Germany. The popular cry across the country will soon be: 'We want eight and we won't wait!'

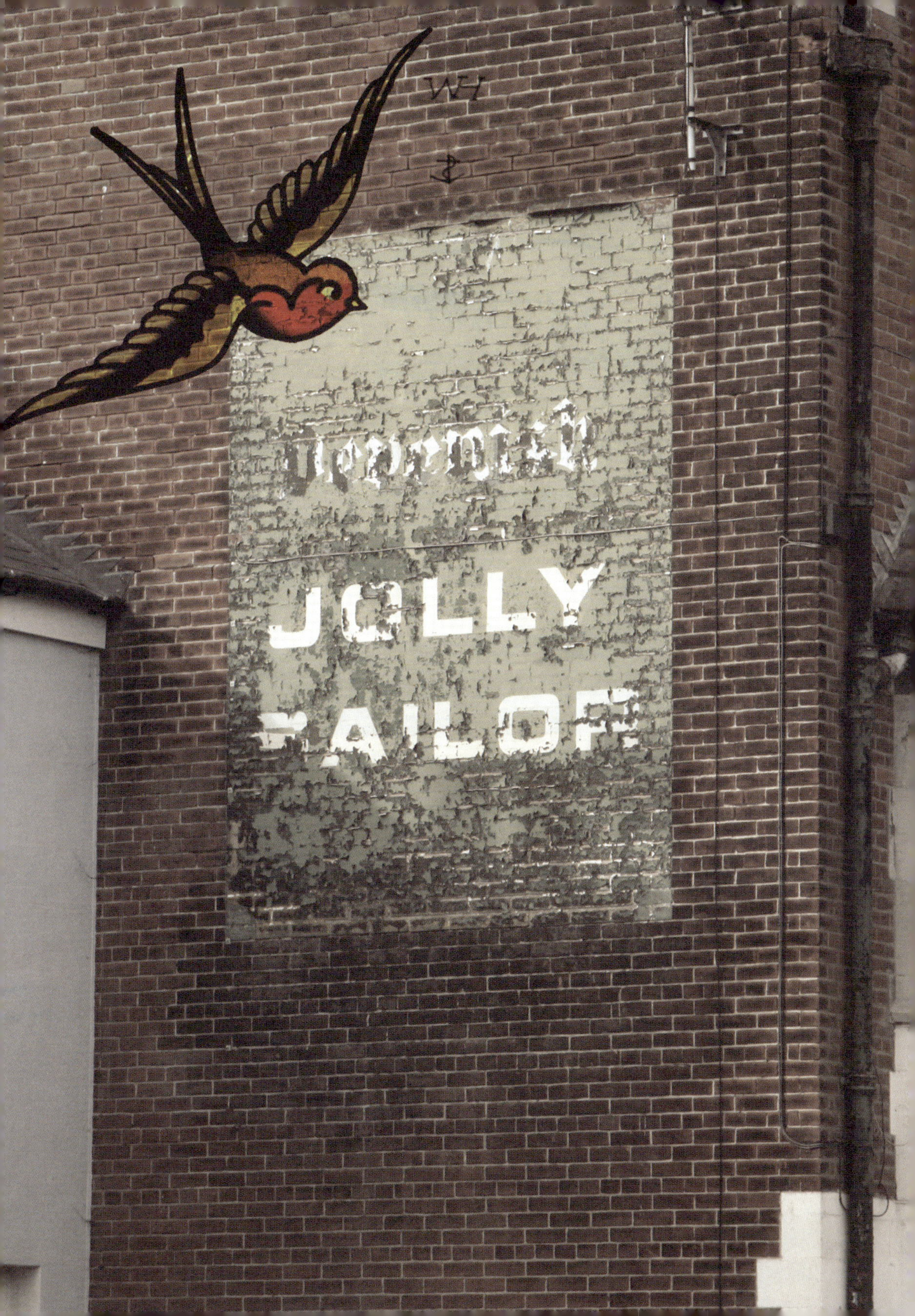
JOLLY

The sea's in my blood. It's a cliche, but true. I know you've got to respect the sea. I've seen it flat, calm. I've seen it a maelstrom. If you take the mick out of it, it will swallow you up. Respect comes from understanding what it can do. It can change in next to no time.

- Andy Straw, Tug Master, Portland Harbour

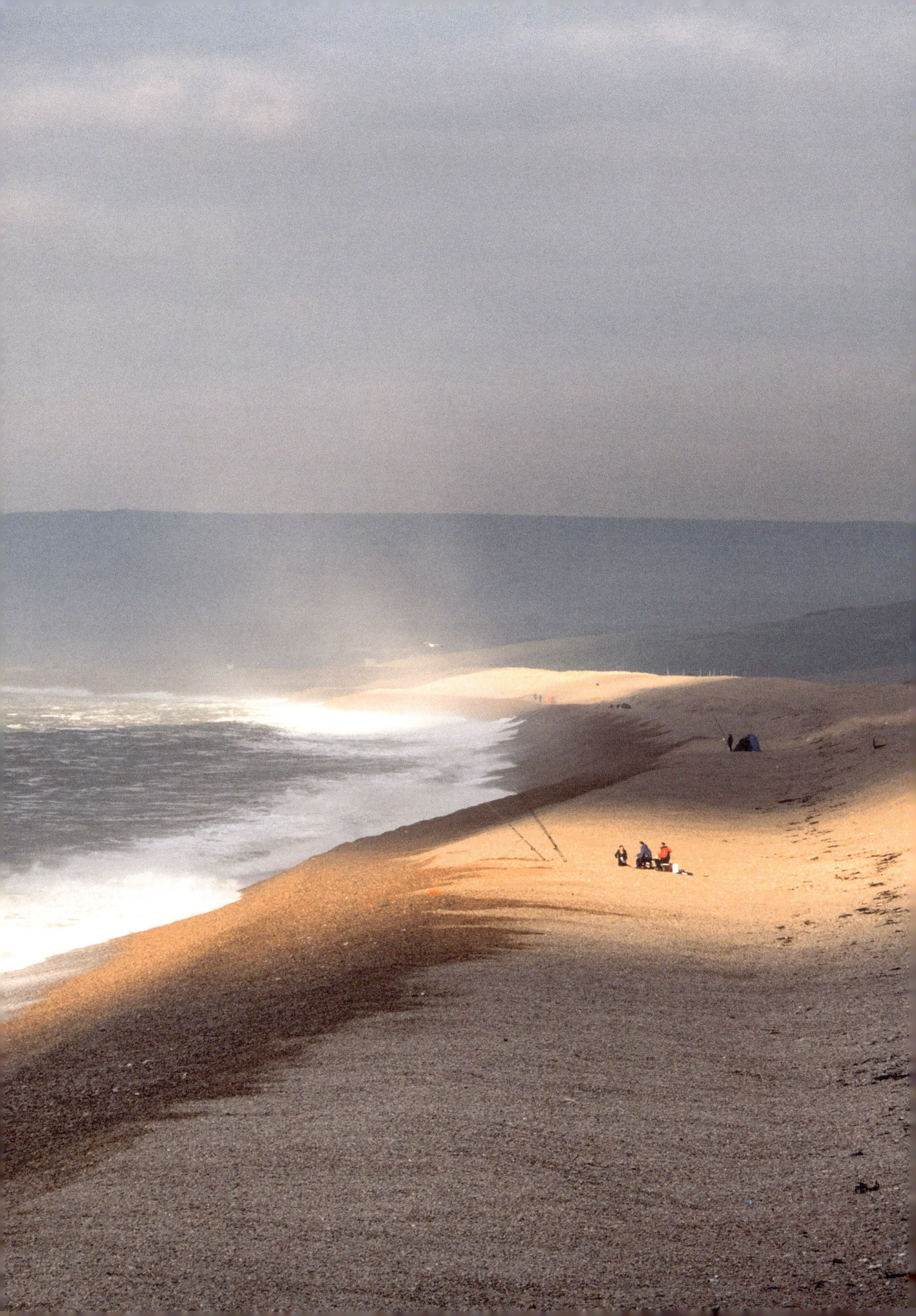

Bill of Portland

WEST INDIES CR		D
PLACE	ARRIVE	
BERMUDA	7 JAN	4
ANTIGUA	12	1
BARBADOS	18	2
GRENADA	22	2
TRINIDAD	29	6
LA GUAIRA	5 FEB	6

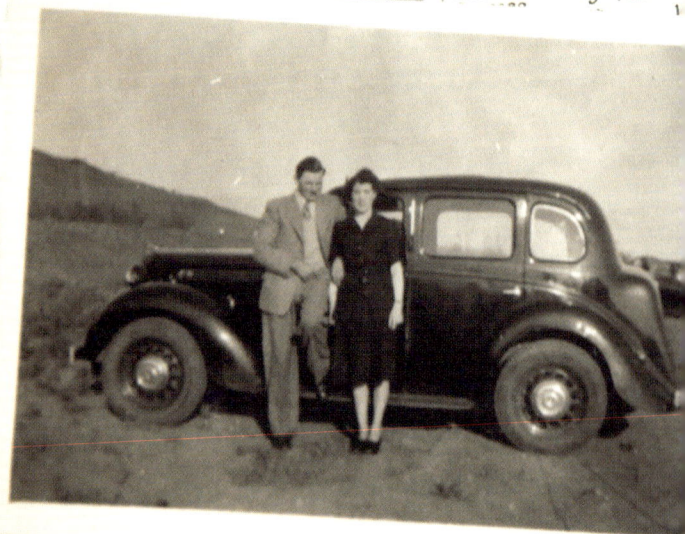

Tá lán mara eileins an fhairge… there is another tide in the sea

Monica Quigley never once regrets coming to live in Dorchester, the county town. The war is over but rationing is still in place. The Atomic Age has dawned. She's the youngest of the litter but not the last one to leave; that will be her brother Séan, who will finally give in to the lure of painting and decorating in London. She first goes to work for Mr Clark of Street, the noted shoe manufacturer, who has been an admirer of the business letters she composes, her politeness and her efficiency in dealing with all correspondence from the leather company in Birr where she was. She wonders if England is full of idiots, if grammar is the measure of a person. But she masks her true feelings, something she will become adept at, composes a reply with the correct tone and so it is his invitation that allows her passage. Since her Da went to the grave she's had itchy feet and Ma won't mind. Ma's got her dogs to look after and her garden to tend and the nuns to gossip with. Ma will be alright, she's as steadfast as they come. Isn't she a woman who encourages her girls to go out in the world and do some good and isn't Ireland a miserable place these days for any youngster with a bit of get up and go? But Monica quickly tires of the same old office work; she looks for a true vocation and finds it in nursing. Her application to train as a State Registered Nurse at Dorset County Hospital is accepted. Days are long and arduous, the Matron strict, but she's earning a wage and has accommodation provided. She enjoys the camaraderie and there's several other Irish lasses here.

Now settled in Dorchester for over 8 years, Sister Quigley goes to work on the Private Ward, where she treats the wives of various entertainers, Admirals and country gentlemen. She has dates with officers of the Fleet, nurses being the first to receive invitations to various Naval Balls and dinners, tennis competitions, skittles evenings and galas, but she declines any solicitations of engagement. They persist. They take her to see 'Old Gravel Throat Himself,' Teddy Foster with his Orchestra, at the Sidney Hall, Weymouth, or to the Ritz Theatre which offers Rosaires International Circus with Lions, Bears, Ponies. She sees Steve Larrabee, who played the Lone Ranger on radio, as he appears in *Mother Goose* at Alexandra Gardens. Wee Georgie Wood takes the lead role, to be whisked away to the Land of Never Never Indians where he is rescued by Steve, who offers a remarkable display of rope wrangling, fancy shooting and cowpoke trickery. There's some nights at the cinema of course, depending on her shifts, with plenty to see – *The Beachcomber*, *The Lawless Breed*, *Lassie Come Home*, *Prince Valiant*, *Tarzan Escapes* or *Calamity Jane*. Now there's a gal! *Above Us The Waves*, with John Mills, has them queuing. It tells the story of the wartime attack on the Tirpitz and is filmed off Portland. The Navy boys lap that one up.

She attends an event in Easton – the wide streets and stone houses there remind her a little of her home town. There is a competition for first aid teams under the direction of Charles Comben, Portland Divisional Superintendent of St Johns Ambulance Brigade. They are required to treat a young cyclist, John White, who has sustained a severe wound to his forearm and a fractured thigh. The injuries have been realistically faked. Staff from Bath & Portland Stone Firm come 6th with a score of 99½, while Weymouth Police take the prize with score of 160. Captain Rudd, one of the surgeons at the Naval Hospital is suitably impressed by the work, as is she. Tea and biscuits are provided for the crowd of spectators. It is a pleasant afternoon's distraction.

There's not a man that can keep me better than I can keep myself, she always says. But in a shoebox she chooses to keep all the letters and photographs that one sailor sends her, which chronicle his cruises. On the back of one photograph he writes: 'Have you forgotten me?' For some years she dates a farmer, and they often go out to Portland for picnics with friends, rambles around the Bill. Invigorating. The keeper of the lighthouse is pleased to show them round, but only in the afternoon, after the lighthouse house keeping chores are all finished. The keeper tells them that before the electricity reached this end of the Isle, the light was turned by a clockwork mechanism. It had to be wound every 75 minutes for 10 minutes and recorded in the logbook, day and night; to fail to wind it is unthinkable, a sackable offence. Illumination was provided originally by oil lamp, the yellowing of the glass caused by the burning of the oil over the years. If the electric supply is lost, he tells them, there is a back up generator. This light was made at a marvellous glassworks in Smethwick, he says.

She doesn't travel too far afield. (She doesn't learn to drive until she's in her 50s.) On days off, walking her dog, she likes to wander the little known roads, known only to lovers, thieves, gypsies, smugglers, ghosts. She exudes a nervous energy; it's rare that she will sit down and read a book. She's as skinny as a rake, she has no need to keep her figure by eating those newfangled starch reduced Energen Rolls the other girls favour. She goes across the Channel on pilgrimage to Lourdes on two occasions, and up to the Midlands now and then to visit family. Adjoining Birmingham, the Black

Country is dingy and grimy. The smell of factories in the air all around, a heavy metallic smell, mixed with the aroma of greased axles, rust, damp air, oil stained brick and concrete, the grinding and cutting and polishing and shaping and pounding and smelting. Everything is grey, brown and blackened. Ireland was greens and glorious blues – even the rain had a sparkle of colour.

At times, the rocky Isle of Portland reminds her of Connemara, home to generations of Quigleys – incredibly beautiful, but you can't eat a vision of a landscape can you? She recalls her Ma's family tales, of scraping a living on rocks, those pocket handkerchief style fields, constantly divided and sub-divided through the families, smaller and smaller strips, simple folk laying seaweed to enrich the few inches of soil, making a living off the crumbs. There's a sense of this harshness here on the Isle, but with plenty of lobsters and crabs nearby and enough willing fellows with their wicker pots to catch them, no-one knows the hunger. Then there's the bay packed with mackerel, men casting out the nets, hauling them in, full of the bounty of the sea.

Sisters and cousins come on vacation, down from the North or the Midlands for a breath of fresh air. Much later she will take me, her nephew and only godchild, to the Bill and the light. 'Not as rough as the Atlantic breakers back home,' she says, looking at the Race a little wistfully. Even though she's not a swimmer, she likes being near the water, feeling that tang of spray in the mouth. At night, as a chill descends, there's a mystery about the sea, with that quilt of stars above. Nobody knows how many stars there are up there. My *I-Spy The Sky* book doesn't tell me. Nobody knows how many lighthouse prisms the glassworks made, nor how many lives are saved by their unique beams of light.

To the seaside

Surrounding us, on every side of Portland, the salty air, the lure of the ocean. Even far inland, as Smethwick is, we are familiar with the call of the briny. The canals built by Brindley, Smeaton and Telford linked to the rivers Severn, Trent and Mersey, a watery route to the coast. The steam trains took us Black Country folk to the seaside to enjoy Bank Holiday weekends away and for the Industrial Fortnight, when the big factories shut down in the last week of July and first week of August. Over the decades, in ever increasingly numbers we took our suitcases to North Wales, the North West, Devon and Dorset, to fill up the burgeoning holiday camps and boarding houses. Weymouth, with its golden sands and its wide bay, was compared by some to the Bay of Naples, not that any of us had ever been there. And across the bay, we could clearly see the Navy base and the brooding Isle itself. Christopher Marsden, writing at the end of the 1940s, cast a cynical eye over proceedings:

'The English can once again resume, where they will, their odd littoral enjoyments. Once again there will be able to fill their hair with salt and their shoes with stones; they will be free once more to migrate to small and rainy towns in trains that are only crowded at the very time they travel; to leave their comfortable homes to eat unlovely meals in lodgings presided over by cross women with fanatical parsimoniousness. They will be permitted again the annual repurchase of pails that do not hold water, of spades that do not dig, of tin moulds more suited to blancmange than to irresolute sand. Once more they will hear the long sagas of boring old salts. The more reasonable sensual pleasures of the seaside will also be open to them; the wriggling of bare toes in sand; the working of depressions for buttocks; the popping of blistered seaweed. They will be able to inhale again in the sunshine that curious aroma, always slightly fecal, which belongs to the rearward parts of beaches – composed of flies and old newspapers and unintentionally dried fish. They will experience again the sensation of hot bathing-huts, like wooden ovens, feeling sandy feet grate on salt wet boards and catching their clothes on unnoticed nails. They will know once more the mottled shudder of goose-flesh. They will cut their feet on glass, tread delicately over shingle, mount smooth concrete promenades to feign the horny feet of seamen.'

"WHO'S A-FEÄRD?"

THE DORSET YEAR BOOK

1904 — JUBILEE YEAR — 1954

In this passage, Marsden is seemingly the inheritor of the beliefs of antiquity, which posited the sea as a wholly unhealthy place. Yet we begin life as waterborne creatures, suspended in the rich amniotic fluid of the womb. With over 60% of our body composed of water – our brain and heart is 73% – an average human being can only survive three days without water. We have an ancient urge to live near it; for sustenance, cleansing, for healing, and – latterly – for a great view.

Our love affair with the seaside itself is a relatively new thing, as for thousands of years we feared the vastness of the sea, resonant of the Biblical flood. Until the mid-18th century, Europeans experienced only dread at the thought of the sea. It was a violent and unpredictable place that threw ships against the rocks, devoured sailors and gave off nauseous and pungent smells. It was also home to monsters. For the Greeks, Scylla and Charybdis awaited foolhardy mariners, as did the Sirens. The Book of Job told of the Kraken and the Leviathan, the Norse had Jörmungandr, China the Shèn, Japan the Ikuchi. The terrible sea brought Viking raiders to the Isle of Portland, the Black Death to Weymouth. While 70% of the earth's surface lies beneath the waters, some 95% of it remains unexplored – it is still a place of unfathomable mystery and wonder, of the Sargasso Sea, the Flying Dutchman, the Mary Celeste, the Bermuda Triangle, lost pirate treasures, the Marianas Trench, Godzilla.

Olive Philpott says that it was only on Portland that she really came to know the sea. Hailing from a village far inland, near the Wiltshire border, she remembers at the age of 6 being struck by a large oil painting in the parlour of a family friend – a magnificent seascape, just sea and sky, no land visible, great turbulent heaving waves. It is on a school trip to Bournemouth where she first encounters the sea in real life, but what a disappointment, not one little bit like her beloved picture. No drama. Flat as a pancake. She just sits on the sand and cries, much to the bafflement of her guardians.

In 1908, when she is 17, her Aunt and Uncle go to live in Weymouth. They take her to Portland to 'see the prisoners.' Going up on that queer little railway that winds up along the side of the cliff, she finds the sight of the convicts working in the quarries quite harrowing and so they quickly move on to Southwell and walk all the way to the Bill. The newly built lighthouse there is quite magnificent and it is here she finally finds the sea of her cherished picture, the sea of her dreams where the great waves dash against mighty cliffs. She writes: 'Here my love for the sea was born, here Portland claimed my heart for ever.' She is told that you can have no halfway feeling about Portland; you either hate it or you love it. 'However that maybe,' she decides, 'I belong to the latter group, for mine was love at first sight and felt an urge to climb to its summit.'

For many years, the Bill remains a wide, lonely open space, 'almost terrifying in its solitary grandeur.' Those blackberries they pick are some of the largest she has ever eaten. She muses on what glorious times the children have amongst the rocks, limpeting, fishing, gathering driftwood to carry home to the winter fires – ship-shoring they call that. 'Sometimes the boys would build themselves little huts with stones, roofing them over with the bits of corrugated iron, sacking, or linoleum, anything they could get hold of, to play in. We can imagine these children pretending to be Excise Men, or smugglers, Red Indians or pirates, in turn, in their happy playtime.' She watches as they swim in the water off Hallelujah Bay, where the big rocks still have texts painted upon them by some religious enthusiast. She observes the fishermen at work, gathering their lobster pots, and sometimes she goes out with them. When the mackerel season comes, she knows to stand on a high cliff. When the sea is ruffled – 'mackell shay' the fishermen call it – the watchers shout that the fish are there and the men shoot out their nets. They keep an eye out for sprats and sand eels breaking the surface – there's a good chance they'll be mackerel underneath. They watch for terns and gannets; if you see them diving, the fish won't be far away. She hears them call a half grown mackerel a 'haymaker,' a rock bream is a 'cunner,' a cuttlefish a 'quiddle,' a spider crab an 'aviar.'

Over the decades she returns many, many times to her perfect picture, though the scenery changes. A road to the Bill is built in the 1920s and the first charabancs begin their journeys, then private motor-cars bring more day-trippers. Replacing the old coastguard cottages, in 1934 a coastguard station is built, near to the old Upper Light (which Marie Stopes uses as her summer residence, still viewed as a controversial character). Olive is 61 years old when, in 1952, The Lobster Pot cafe opens next door to the lighthouse to service the increase in visitors. A few years later the Devenish Arms opens, a little further up. Some of the fisherman huts begin to be used as holiday chalets, though the Red Crane stills hauls up working boats. The old Lower Light becomes a bird observatory. The Admiralty construct some ugly buildings for some kind of test or other – all very secretive. The wildness and sense of solitude can still be found, but in the out of season months. One day an old fisherman tells Olive, 'Miss, if you do come here much more, we shall feel as if you are one o' we.' What a tremendous compliment, she tells herself.

John Piper first comes to Portland Bill in the late 1920s – 'in a very old Morris Cowley' – and is enthralled by the visual untidyness of the place, the magnificent disarray of the low quarry shores, the scattering of fishermen huts, the dominance of the lighthouse. He too will return many times. He writes: 'I am a map-lover and Portland looks too extraordinary for words on the map, so does the adjoining Chesil Beach.' He describes the character of the island as being 'large-scale, airy, maritime, naval, above all workaday, and not picturesque, except by accident.' He paints the local scenes with oil on board or canvas or linen, all shapes and sizes. He uses gouache, watercolour, pen and ink. He takes with him to the coast a folder with coloured papers, which he cuts and tears into shapes to create landscapes in situ, adding paint and ink. He is interested in the 'vernacular types of buildings that histories and historians for the most part ignored.' For him this includes pubs, non-conformist chapels, country railway stations and lighthouses. As the 1950s begins, he finds the foreshore more ship-shape, thronged with holidaymakers; still, he sketches and paints, noting, 'The sea is the mystery that lies beyond the flat fields and the woods and downs, the rough moors and the Black Country recesses: never far away.'

Uriah William George Mitchell, or just Bill to his friends, is a quarryman. The only time he leaves the island is to go away to the Second World War. Surrounded by the sea all of his life, he knows he's a terrible sailor but, as he has spent some time with the St Johns Ambulance, he puts in a request to serve in the Army Medical Corps. Instead the powers that be decide to stick him on a Red Cross ship, so it's a life on the ocean wave for him. It's here he meets and befriends a chap who happens to come from the distant Black Country. They spend the entire war in each other's company, on that ship. The Black Country fellow promises, if they make it through to the end, then he will bring his whole family down to Portland to visit Bill for their holidays. *Gooin' t' the Bill t' visit Bill.* It's something to dream about in those tough years. And that's exactly what happens, though the way Bill describes it, these Black Country folk think they're coming to some tropical paradise like Hawaii. Although it certainly isn't that, the Isle soon casts its magic spell over them and every summer they return, as do many holidaymakers from their neck of the woods. To top it all, Bill's oldest son, David, who's training to be a draughtsman, falls in love with their youngest daughter Tanis. Once she's turns 18, she moves down from the West Midlands to Portland. They marry and have three boys.

Another Portlander who went to the war is now sent to prison for 12 months after breaking and entering a house in Weymouth. 32-year-old Ronald Tucker is already on probation after 2 previous similar charges, and he admits to another offence in Dorchester. As a 15-year-old, he began work in the quarries, then serves for six years as a trooper in the Royal Armoured Corps. He sees action in North Africa and Italy, is blown up and hospitalised a number of times. He returns to work in the quarries a changed man; now a heavy drinker, he misses work a number of times. His nerves are said to be in a shocking condition. He drinks, he tells the court, because he's bothered by nightmares and cannot sleep. His solicitor asks the court to consider some long medical course for him, but the court state they neither have the power nor the appropriate knowledge to order such a thing.

The Navy remains the significant presence on the island, after the long defence of Britain in the recent war and as a key point of embarkation for over 500,000 troops and 140,000 vehicles during the D-Day invasion. Ten reinforced concrete caissons, built as part of Mulberry harbours to support the Normandy landings, lie in Portland Roads, towed back across the Channel. Eight are given to the Netherlands to help repair breached dykes in 1953, two remaining as a windbreak for the piers. Helicopters are now operating from the base's playing fields. The Admiralty Gunnery Establishment has been built at Southwell. After stiff local opposition, the Air Ministry drops plans to extend combat ranges with a ground to air firing range at Chesil Beach; the Admiralty states that most of their gunnery activities on their range will be 'silent or non-firing' and the interference to amenities only occasional.

The Admiralty own the Portland Breakwater Lighthouse, though Trinity House provide the 3 keepers. The light is surrounded by some utilitarian brick buildings which sit at the end of the breakwater, which provide sparse accommodation. There's an air raid shelter which has been converted into a coal store and oil store. The tower is a metal tube about 6 feet in diameter, supported by vertical girder work. At the top, the tube opens out into the lantern. It was all made in Smethwick, first recorded in the Chances Order book of 1903: *'9th March. Portland Breakwater Lighthouse on Head A. Iron lighthouse tower 52 feet high consisting of cast iron columns and steel bracings, together with central tube and Lantern Gallery. All to drawings and specifications. Testing of materials will be done by an inspector from Admiralty at our works. Delivered complete by end of June next.'* It carries a Third Order optic, one designed for use in harbours. The clock mechanism has a small spindle, which takes an inordinate amount of time to wind up; over 800 turns and then it only runs for about an hour and a quarter. The keepers must climb the tower every 2 hours during the night to wind the mechanism and pump the oil up to the lamp. There are a lot of rats to chase away. There are various dismantled buildings along the breakwater formerly used by the coastal defences to poke about in, plenty of warships and submarines to have a look at. The only good thing to be really said about it is that you can easily get ashore, early in the mornings if you need fresh meat and vegetables, thanks to the use of the harbour master's launch.

A sailing guide to the south coast tells yacht owners that the harbour here is 'by no means devoid of interest and attraction and in some ways is preferable to Weymouth' – though strangers must remember that this is a Navy port with numerous floating targets, mooring buoys and a torpedo testing range. Red flags are flown during practice and a shrill whistle warns of the discharge of a torpedo. They can find a landing stage at Old Castle Cove, where there is a sailing club, with water from a tap available. There is also water to be had at Castletown, or from a water lighter. A post office and shops can be found here, with early closing day Wednesdays. Only HM ships are allowed to anchor east of a line running north near the Kings Harbour Master's office, as defined by two white obelisks ashore.

The Admiralty announce they will be putting 174 houses to accommodate ratings on the Verne. They are also building a testing facility at the Bill on land within an area of former quarries (which will later become part of their Underwater Weapons Establishment). Raymond C. Morris, of Chamberlaine Road, writes a number of letters of complaint about these developments. He is concerned that the area of open grassland has been drastically reduced and natural scenery is all but non-existent. 'The Bill of Portland is still there,' he admits, 'but its true character has gone. What remains but brick and chain-link fencing?' He points out that there has been no public body challenging the Admiralty. 'Does this public apathy indicate that in the face of constant and insatiable demands from government departments for more and more land, the public has reached a level of complete subservience. If this is so, what thanks shall we deserve from the future generations, when they receive their inheritance a grievously mutilated England.' Surely this is democracy gone crazy! A valuable local amenity is in the process of destruction. He continues: 'Anyone who has visited the Bill recently will know that this fear has now been realised. Contractors have started their work and are busy building in brick in addition to making extensive excavation. Scenically the result of their labours is appalling. The whole western vista, from the Old Lighthouse southwards, is completely spoilt. Despite an Admiralty statement suggesting otherwise, the 10 ft security fence has NOT been curtailed to give access to the cliff path. The enclosure is within a few yards of the famous Pulpit Rock and has succeeded in spoiling the scenic amenity of this well known and much appreciated beauty spot as well as depriving holidaymakers and other visitors of the recreational use of a large expanse of open grassland.'

In February 1955, a 19 year old Navy cook, Archibald Knox Fraser Duff, is charged with murder of a shipmate at Portland Police station, after a stabbing aboard his frigate moored alongside the coaling pier. He had been drinking at the Breakwater Hotel and continued drinking back on the ship. According to a witness, an indecent comment started the affray. When cautioned the cook said, 'What can I say? I must have been mad. I hate the Navy. I want to get out and work for a living.' Another witness alleged he confessed, 'I have stabbed a man. I felt it go in. I will hang for this. At least I'll get out of this mob. Finished.' Duff also asked, 'Can I get a cup of tea before I hang, Chief?' He did not hang and defence records of the trial remain closed until 2056. In June, another tragedy, as the submarine Sidon sinks in the harbour. A faulty torpedo explodes in the tubes, immediately killing 13 sailors. An eye-witness reports: 'A sheet of flame shot up through the conning tower, followed by another sheet of flame and with it pieces of equipment and furniture, hats and coats were flung into the air.' A week later, it takes 21 hours to salvage the vessel. Comedian Norman Wisdom leads a celebrity concert at the Alexandra Gardens Theatre in aid of dependents. The boat is eventually refloated and used for target practice.

At the annual dinner of the Portland branch of the Civil Service Clerical Association, the Captain-In-Charge of the Naval base, Captain G. M. Sladen tells them that without the Navy this country 'may as well just pack up.' He says that no matter how many atom bombs are dropped on this country there still will be a great many people left on these isles and their wants would still have to be provided for and brought across the sea. He tells them: 'In the last day or two there has been a letter in the press saying that the Air Force can supply all the defences of the country today. Anyone who believes that is just a fool. They have no idea of the true state of affairs.'

In July, 3,000 U.S. sailors come ashore to celebrate their Independence Day and are on their best behaviour. The aircraft carrier New Jersey, destroyers R.L. Wilson and Basilone with their supply ship Salamone, arrive at the naval base on the morning of 4th July to enjoy local hospitality. Special

PERHAPS IT WAS TOO HOT: Despite the exceptional weather only 5,916 people attended the first of two Portland Navy Days on Saturday Compared with last year, when it was not quite so hot, this figure is down by nearly half. In this 'Echo' picture two ratings from the Portchester Castle are showing two attractive young visitors, Geraldine Sowerby (left) and Pauline Reed, of Dagenham, the workings of the ship's control dances and entertainments are arranged for them, with fireworks across the bay at 10.30 pm. Their officers attend a cocktail party at the residence of the Captain-in-Charge.

By the end of that month, hotels are fully booked, thousands of tin buckets and spades have been purchased, and postcards sell like hotcakes. The shutdown of the factories in the West Midlands brings even more crowds. One young couple tell Mr J. Stone from the Dorset Daily Echo that they think it's quite wonderful here. They've been swimming and fishing and walking to Osmington Mills and from the Bill to Church Ope Cove. Everything is light and colour, the air crisp and fresh. Some older couples say there's not much to do in the evening, at least not as much as in the good old days of music hall.

A Weymouth councillor, Mr J. R. Tudor Griffith, suggests that the area needs an airport at Warmwell and more helicopter landing grounds to attract tourists. He worries that the local entertainments will suffer in the face of competition from the coming of the television. 'What we need,' he suggests, 'is a massive Dreamland amusement centre.' Nevertheless, it proves to be a record bank holiday on 1st August, the hottest for 9 years. All the talk of H-bomb tests, supersonic bangs and such things spoiling the weather is now forgotten. 25,000 postcards are collected at the weekend, and another 20,000 on Monday; most are going back to the Midlands. There are no tickets to be had for the extra trains to and from Wolverhampton – all reservations have gone.

The Navy Open Day at the base on Saturday attracts 5,916 people, down by nearly half on the previous year; this is blamed on the heat, though 8,000 do turn up on the Monday. It's standing room only for Harry Hudson at the Pier Bandstand, while over 500 people pay to play 'gadget golf' and 57,372 deckchairs are hired out on the sands. The consequent litter on the streets has to be seen to believed, ankle deep in places, complains one person who signs themselves as 'Forty Years A Ratepayer.' The South Portland Branch of the South Dorset Conservative Association are also concerned about the accumulating litter at Portland Bill and the poor impression it must give to visitors. 'A dilapidated car park, totally inadequate public conveniences and out of date methods of obtaining drinking water,' they say, pointing their finger at the council. One local resident on Portland puts the blame elsewhere. S.A. writes: 'The Bill is a disgrace, but if there were bins every few yards there still would be litter, I've heard people say how disgusting it is – and then drop litter themselves. There is a good waste bin in the bus shelter at Fortune's Well, but the floor is usually covered in litter, I notice! Until pockets are touched we shall have litter. How many people put their used bus tickets in the bus boxes? They throw them on the pavement.'

There is a new attraction. A bird observatory has been established at the RN wireless telegraphy station at the Bill. Portland Bird Observatory holds an open day, with 30 visitors observing the trapping and ringing of migrant birds. The chair of the new Observatory Committee, Dr K. B. Rooke, had started with a caravan in the autumn of 1951, setting up a trap at Culverwell. So far over 1,300 birds of 42 species have been ringed up to the previous year, but this year alone they have ringed 700 birds from 33 species. He hopes there can be a more permanent facility on the Isle, as ornithology is becoming popular and the Bill attracts a great range of birds. Recently, five new species have been observed: a Melodious Warbler, Red-breasted Flycatcher, Pied Wheatear, Bonelli's Warbler and Orphean Warbler.

There is concern about peacocks of a different plumage. Several Weymouth lads, described in court as Teddy Boys, are charged with stealing beer from a hotel. People are advised by the local press to be on the alert for the following: men wearing narrow trousers, only 14-16 inches wide at the bottom compared with the normal 21 inches; loose fitting jackets, two or three inches longer than the usual, with extra long lapels; narrow black ties; white shirts and white socks; the trousers usually black or very dark grey and the jackets either matching or in very light shades. Clothing like this is actually quite hard to find in Weymouth or Portland. 'I expect the lads get their outfits in Bournemouth,' says the manager of one large shop. Nevertheless, naval and army ratings are checked before leaving camp to ensure their trousers are more than 17 inches at the turn up and their jackets are not inclined to drape. Some National Servicemen have been seen about the town wearing colourful shirts.

William John Mills, aged 23, a labourer of Harbour View Road, is charged with damaging a mirror valued at £2 7s 6d at a dance at Portland Drill Hall. Inspector Payne comments: 'This man is one of the very few in Portland, I am glad to say, who dresses in a peculiar manner and seems to think there is no code of behaviour to which they have to conform, and who do cause a little trouble around the dance hall.' Wills offered no explanation in court. The chairman, Mr P. H. Allen, tells him: 'This offence is not the sort of thing to be passed over lightly. You go to a dance and make a nuisance of yourself so you have got to pay for it.' He is fined £5, ordered to pay full damages and 2s costs within 4 weeks. No doubt some Portlanders will remind us of the good old days when, in 1817, John Flann, a 20-year-old, was convicted of being 'a Rogue and a Vagabond, and pretending to crafty science and representing himself as a wizard, to the great disturbance of the peace of the inhabitants of Portland.'

There are a plethora of post-war publications marketed to holidaymakers. *The Countryside and How to Enjoy It* (1948) gives clear instructions: 'Make room in your pocket for a bird book, carry field glasses, and have a camera always at the ready. And never start out without an inch to the mile ordnance map mounted on linen and cut into sections. Keep this map in a military leather map case which can be easily slung over your shoulders and carried in comfort.' They encourage the reader to walk the landscape to find a 'land of a beauty so quiet and so subtle that those who live in the noise and bustle of the towns may rightly take it as a foretaste of heaven. It is the source of British greatness, and will be the source of happiness to you lasting for the rest of your life.' Then they admonish: 'If your legs and feet cannot cope with countryside walking, it is because they have been allowed to fall into disuse. When climbing, shorten your pace and follow the natural tendency to bend your knees and incline your body forward. It is a mistake to stride out with great speed in an effort to get it over and done with. In descending steeply, the knees should still be bent, but the body inclined backward as though sitting on nothing. It is a good plan, going downhill, to let oneself go, with short zig-zag runs. This prevents complete loss of leg control.' A true Portlander will not be needing this kind of advice.

As for the quarries, that other unique feature of the Isle, there's been a boom on – with great demand for use in post-war rebuilding programmes. Plymouth City Centre, flattened by German bombs in 1941, is rebuilt using Portland stone. South Western Stone Company at Easton are busy promoting Stonetex, reconstituted natural stone building blocks 'with all the attributes of natural stone which brings a new home within the reach of Mr Everyman's pocket.' These are made by crushing natural stones and reconstituted with cement, making it stronger and more water resistant than the original stone.

Portland Council have made a controversial order stopping quarrying on the edge of a residential zone in New Street, Easton, while they also discuss the building of houses on 171 acres on virgin quarry land, something opposed by local stone firms, who argue it will shorten the life of their industry by 100 years. Some councillors agree that the area of quarrying and yielding block stone is becoming dangerously low. Councillor Coombe states that a man of 30 can no longer look forward to a life-time of occupation in the trade, though Councillor Packer thinks this a red herring, saying that even Wren advanced the same kind of argument. 'I am surprised to hear that sob stuff,' adds Councillor Pike. Others thought you could live to the age of Methuselah before the supply of stone would be exhausted. In May 1955, they then give outline approval for caravan sites at East and West Weares, despite one council member objecting: 'I have never heard of such a hideous thing in my life.' The general feeling is that people have a liking for sea air and one should not ignore the many thousands coming to Portland Bill during the summer months. In these congested British Isles, such natural advantages mean tourists, and tourists mean money.

As Skylark Durston walks the whole of the island, he wonders what happened to the old quarry bells that he would hear on his way to school, that signaled each working day. It seems so long since he heard even a single

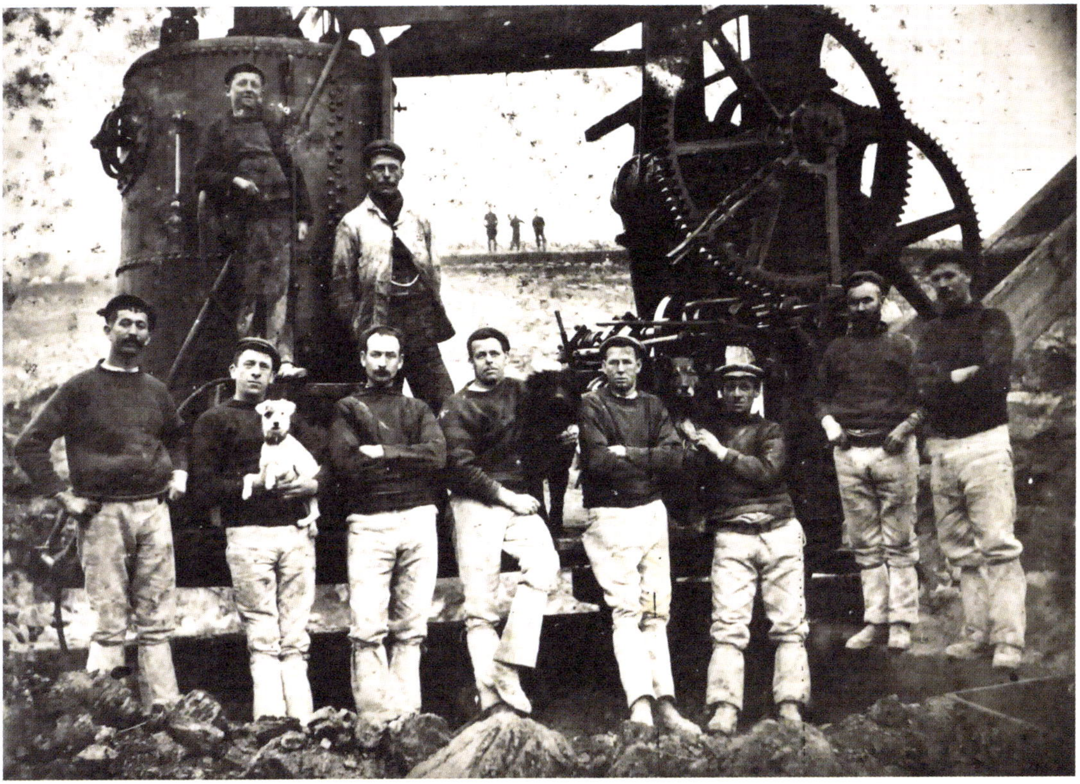

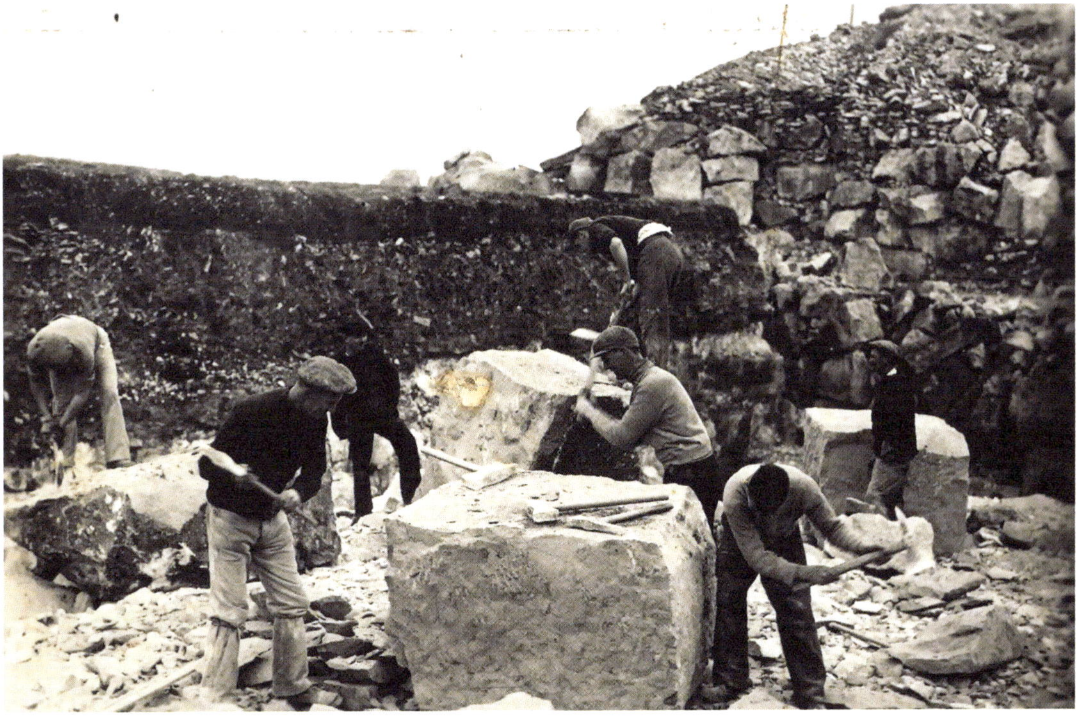

roundelay. The times are changing, there's no doubt, the old giving way to the new, things seeming to have accelerated since the end of the war. Born in 1910, he's in his mid-forties now, as the South Western Stone Company give a trial run to the biggest circular saw in the world. It's 11 feet by 7½ inches, with a cutting edge of 300 rectangular sockets, which hold 270 diamonds as well as 30 clusters of smaller diamonds. The saw operates at the equivalent of 120 mph and can cut through a block of Portland stone 4 foot thick in under 10 minutes, something which would normally take 10 hours by frame sawing. He's amazed at the noise these big saws make, how they can run day and night; he supposes this is the only way they can pay for themselves. Then there's the introduction of smaller saws that can cut with unerring precision. So clean, concise and so straight, they can even cut at angles. It's a revolution of a kind, as ancient skills become redundant. The company say, 'No-one will be put out of work, as the men will be absorbed into other essential work here.' But still Skylark wonders how these new-fangled machines might usurp the old crafts. How long before there is no more back-breaking, sinew straining work some 60 feet down in the ground, where even now he can hear the clink of the hammers as they drive metal spikes into the stone?

He was born within sight of these quarries and the sea. He played here as a child, amidst the piles of stones and below the cliffs, walked where he wanted. There were no fences then. Quarrymen at work, stout fellows, some as big as Charles Atlas, working in pairs to split the rock along the seam, taking turns to drive in the wedges with heavy sledgehammers, keeping time with a chant or a singsong. He still relishes this sense of freedom, to wander the Isle, even when it's cold and bleak, shrouded in mist. It's then that the muse hits him and he wants to write poetry. He sits down, strikes a match, lights a fag, watches the sea and all its moods, writes a note: 'loveliness on the morning tide, cheerful and endless.'

As an apprentice stonemason, he learned how to interpret the drawings on paper with the skill in his hands. He says the stones have always talked to him. Alongside him were 70 masons, who sang to the beat of the hammer and the mallet. As he worked to embellish the rock, he whistled all the time; then his foreman said, 'We've got a bloody Skylark here.' The name sticks.

Old habits die-hard, all that is left sometimes is a memory

As the 1950s begin Janet Cartwright is 8 years old. The King is still on the stamps as she writes to her father Frank. Her letters describe her day-to-day doings, the Brownies, schoolwork, losing her milk teeth, passing her exams. Before she can shape words, she draws him pictures. They are still using ration books in Smethwick, so when he returns from his engineering duties he brings a box of fresh groceries from his lighthouse allowance – and jam. She has never seen such a large jar of jam. Sometimes he is away for months on end. A letter takes more than a week to get there, a week to get back. He is all over the place. He's was once out in the West Indies, where he was caught in a hurricane and lucky to get home again.

He's been to the Middle East, Kish Bank and Skerryvore in the Irish Sea, to the Hebrides, Orkneys and Shetlands, John O'Groats, Mallair Harbour, Beachy Head, the Needles, St. David's Head. He tells her about driving out to a lighthouse in the middle of nowhere when the driver suddenly stops, gets out and kneels on a mat for his prayers. You don't see that every day. On that job, he has to make his own knife and fork, as they eat with their hands in those parts. And there's no machinery, they have to pull the stuff up with a rope. He says the land lights are the easy ones to service, though one winter he is working at Dunnet Head in Scotland when he falls down the steps and ends up in hospital for Hogmanay.

Birthday cards arrive from exotic locations, India, Gibraltar. There's no telephone, no email, only paper, stamps and envelopes. She asks him to send as many stamps as possible, so she can split them amongst her friends. They do well collecting stamps; often they fill the surface of the envelopes which hold the precious correspondence to her mother Beatrice and herself. When he's at home, they go on holiday to Torquay, Blackpool, Weston, by coach and train. Truth is, he doesn't really want to be away once he's come back to Topsham Road.

One morning, before she leaves for Holly Lodge school, he tells her he will be testing the foghorns in the afternoon and to listen out for it. When it goes off, she jumps up and shouts, 'That's me Dad!' Nobody else is prepared for it. They are making cookery aprons. It's a huge noise. It stops and then goes again. The teacher gives her a look then explains to the class how the machine that makes that special noise will be fixed on a lighthouse that will be out in the sea, a matter of life or death to the seafarer. Some people at the works call it 'The Grunt.' A few days before testing a new foghorn at

Chances, Barbara Adams, who works in the despatch office at the lighthouse works, is sent out with a couple of other girls into the immediate residential area around the factory perimeter to deliver notices to local households which tells them when the fog horn is to be tested. They also offer to give out sets of earplugs.

There are two different types of horns they test. The bigger of the two is a vertical resonator with the mushroom top, which is supplied to light-vessels and rock islands where an all-round sound is required. The other type is a curved resonator with a jointed trumpet, more akin to a conventional horn; the upper section can be turned downwind when necessary. Each foghorn has its own signature voice – the one at Portland Bill blasts every 30 seconds for 3½ seconds, a type F diaphone, a powerful low frequency tone that can be heard up to ten miles away. Holly Lodge school is only a mile away from the glassworks, so 'The Grunt' provides an astonishing bellow. Janet will later visit some of the locations her father worked – Portland Bill, Corbiere,

Europa Point. She takes the letters to show the keepers. Some do remember him, this meticulous lighthouse engineer and they tell her of his joy when he received one of her letters, postmarked Smethwick, home of the light. She never visits the interior of the Chances factory itself, but she attends children's parties at the Recreation Ground.

The glassworks are slowly adapting back to a peacetime economy. Lighthouse work virtually ceased during the war years, the factory using its expertise to produce searchlights, predictors, sound locators, radar equipment, gun pedestals, reflector floodlights, aerial beacons and buoy lenses. In 1945 Pilkington Brothers of St Helens, for so long a rival glass company, acquire a 50% holding in the company; by 1951 Chance Brothers become a wholly owned subsidiary of Pilkington. The south side of the works are now being modernised, with new products introduced, such as soda lime tubing for fluorescent lights, cathode ray tubes for televisions and radar installations. Sir Hugh Chance, the Chairman, notes that, rather like in the late 30s, rearmament offers new fields of activity, contracts to supply searchlights, mobile floodlighting sets for aerodromes and stand-by generating sets. Another project now being fully developed by the Lighthouse Department is the manufacture of the Sumo Submersible pump.

The BBC Industrial Correspondent, Bertrand Mycock, visits the factory for a broadcast, commenting on its distance from the sea, then stating: 'If you want a lighthouse anywhere in the world, the people of Smethwick will not only make the light, but will plan the tower, tell you where it should stand, and, if you like, will even arrange to build it. But this factory in Smethwick makes other things besides lighthouses. It makes the lenses for car headlamps and railway signals; it gives eyes to the tank driver, the gunner, and the airman. It makes lights for streets and public buildings; it makes tumblers and fruit bowls and test tubes. It made, 100 years ago, a million square feet of glass to the Crystal Palace. It gave Big Ben his shining clock face.'

He notices the little communities of men and woman, each working around their own furnace or workshop, the Black Country bonhomie. He finds the mix of old and new fascinating; some people talk of electronics and radar, alongside those whose craft owes its lineage to the Roman occupation, though he might be left baffled by some of the local dialect:

Moach – to idle about
Myther – to bother, irritate
Nogman – ignoramus

Blaberen – to talk idly (i.e. 'What's her blaberen about?')
Codge – to patch up in an untidy manner (i.e. 'It's a codged job.')

They tell him, half-jokingly, that the factory is basically run by five families. Many of the skills have been handed down the generations, working with some machinery for grinding and polishing that has been running for nearly a century. He watches as a man with a long blowpipe strides up to the furnace, thrusts in the rod, twists it a few times, draws out a blob a glass – 'glowing a milky pink in the gloom.' Swinging it as he goes, giving it a few puffs to expand it, he walks quickly to a pit and lowers it, as an operator below closes a mould around it, then 'the mould is opened and out comes the perfect shape – red now, and yet sparkling...' (He doesn't mention that Chances have provided all the glass globes for Piccadilly Circus.)

He likens the rolling of glass to biscuit making, the flow of molten glass, rolled and patterned, going through ovens whose job is to cool it slowly, then a man cracking it into sheets with a diamond, throwing away the waste pieces with a tremendous crash, a man with a broom handle breaking it up into smaller pieces, those to be reused. Ray Drury, an apprentice draughtsman at this time, describes the rolling machine to be like a massive wringer with all sorts of complications built in. 'The bottom roller had the pattern on and the top roller was smooth,' he says. 'The glass came out of the furnace with the consistency of treacle and went between the rolls. It could not be touched or it would mark so it was supported on a cushion of air until it had set and then it was onto asbestos rolls to travel through an annealing lehr. Out the open it was cooled and then cut and carried off.'

Mycock observes as two men build the gunmetal frame of the optic for a lighthouse bound for Ceylon, which will hold scores of prisms and reflectors to gather up the light and throw it out in a straight and powerful beam. Each must be set at just the right angle. It's a painstaking process that will last three months. He spots a huge piece of optical glass on the floor, like 'an enormous uncut diamond, picking up the light from an open door, and sparkling and flashing, although it was dull and foggy outside.' Ernie Barratt, one of those men, is soon off to Columbo, to spend another four months installing the equipment at Galbokka Point, replacing the old Clock Tower (whose light is now obscured by city buildings). At 95 feet tall, the new light is one third the size and weight of the old tower lamp but is far more powerful. It does not require mercury and, as it works electrically, it only needs one man on watch. Around its concrete base are placed four statues of lions. Meanwhile, N.T. Dalton and M.C. Hitchcox have installed

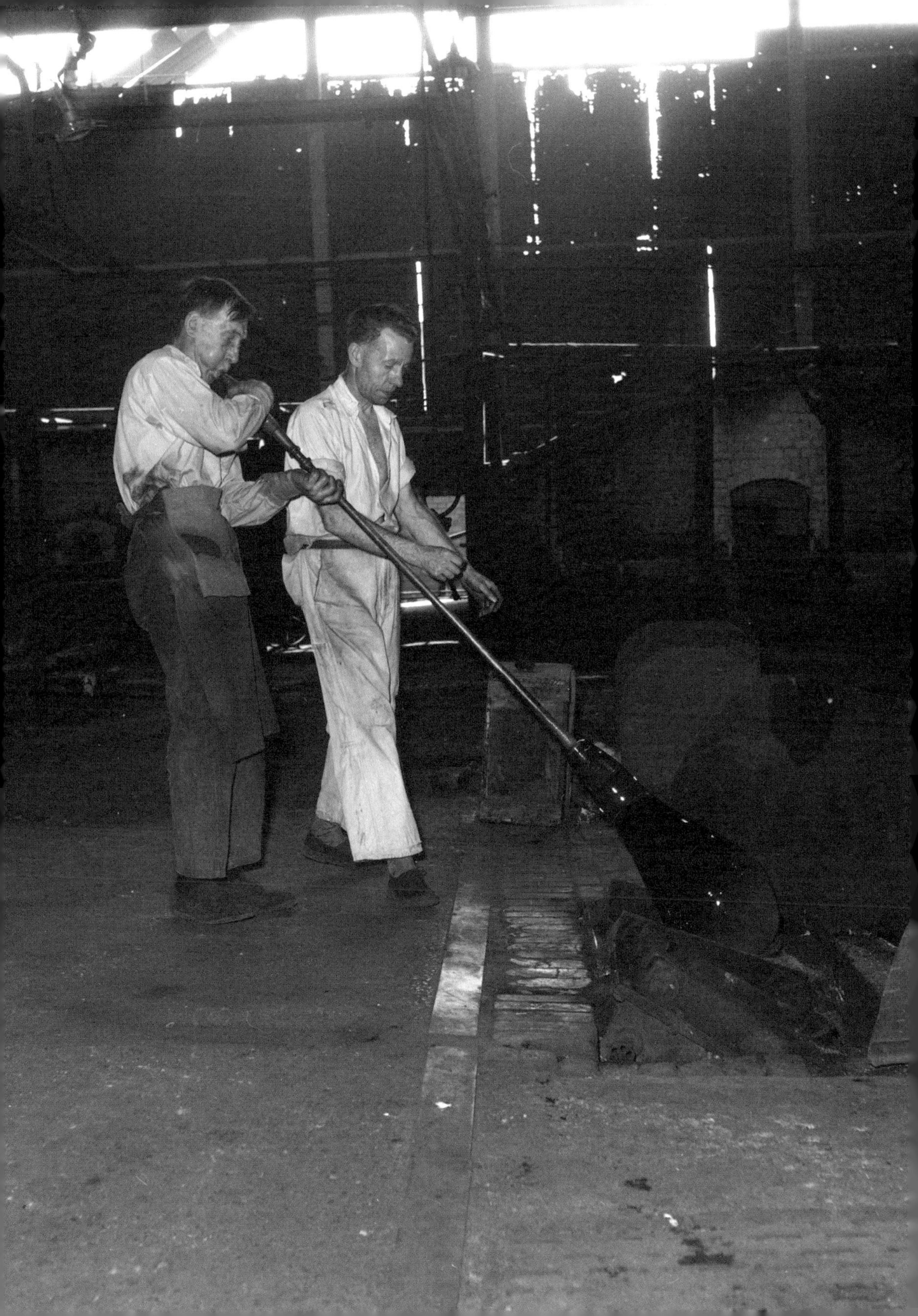

the first lighthouse in Nigeria, at Escravos, atop a steel tower, then one at Bonny River, where the oil industry is developing; then they move on to the Gold Coast for another five installations. Busy times.

In 1951 Chances celebrate the 100th anniversary of their lighthouse works with a rather lavish dinner at the Savoy in London. Things are going well. Exports total 25% of the company's overall turnover, going to 75 countries. Sir John Lang, Permanent Secretary to the Board of the Admiralty, leads the toasts, firstly to the King and then to Chance Brothers themselves and their designers and craftsmen. Sir Hugh Chance replies to the toast, noting it is a curious coincidence that a product requiring the highest degree of reliability should be connected to the name of Chance. There are 300 guests; each of the 34 tables is named after a lighthouse, and each has a host from the company. The decorations are green and red, representing port and starboard lights. The menu has a glass cover with an image of James Timmins Chance and a lighthouse engraved upon it. The menu for the event offers: *Le Saumon Fume*; *La Tortue Verte En Tasse Au Sherry*; *Le Paillettes Au Parmesan*; *Le Fillet De Sole Trouvillaise*; *Le Dindonneau Roti Washington*; *Le Pommes Berny*; *Le Petit Pois Fins*; *L'Ananas Voilee Sultane*; *Les Friandises*; *Le Café*. The wines include: *Amontillado*; *Leibfraumilch aus dem Klosterkeller 1945*; *Chateau Ducru Beaucaillou 1943*; along with *Courvoisier V.S.O.P* and *Liqueurs*. The menu selection is framed by small ink drawings of various ships alongside a mermaid, who is pictured holding up a glass, and Neptune who is holding a cigar as well as his trident. There's even a quote from Longfellow.

You won't find anything quite as posh as that back at the canteen in Spon Lane, Smethwick (though they do provide quantity, some 175,000 hot meals a year). They are still referred to as the New Canteens, even though they have been there for over 35 years. Here, boys and girls under 16 can obtain a full midday meal at a reduced price of 6d. There are some recreation rooms over the canteens, which offer billiard and snooker at midday and week nights.

Their centenary coincides with the Festival of Britain Celebration in London, on the South Bank site. Here the focal point is the old Shot Tower on top of which is placed a Chance Third Order lighthouse optic, with a beam intensity of 3,000,000 candles, 100 times the power of their very first lens at the Great Exhibition. It is operated solely by VHF radio from their London office. Above the optic is a 30-foot diameter aerial of a radio telescope, rotated from the Outer Space section in the Dome of Discovery – here visitors can transmit radio signals to the moon. In this Dome, Chance

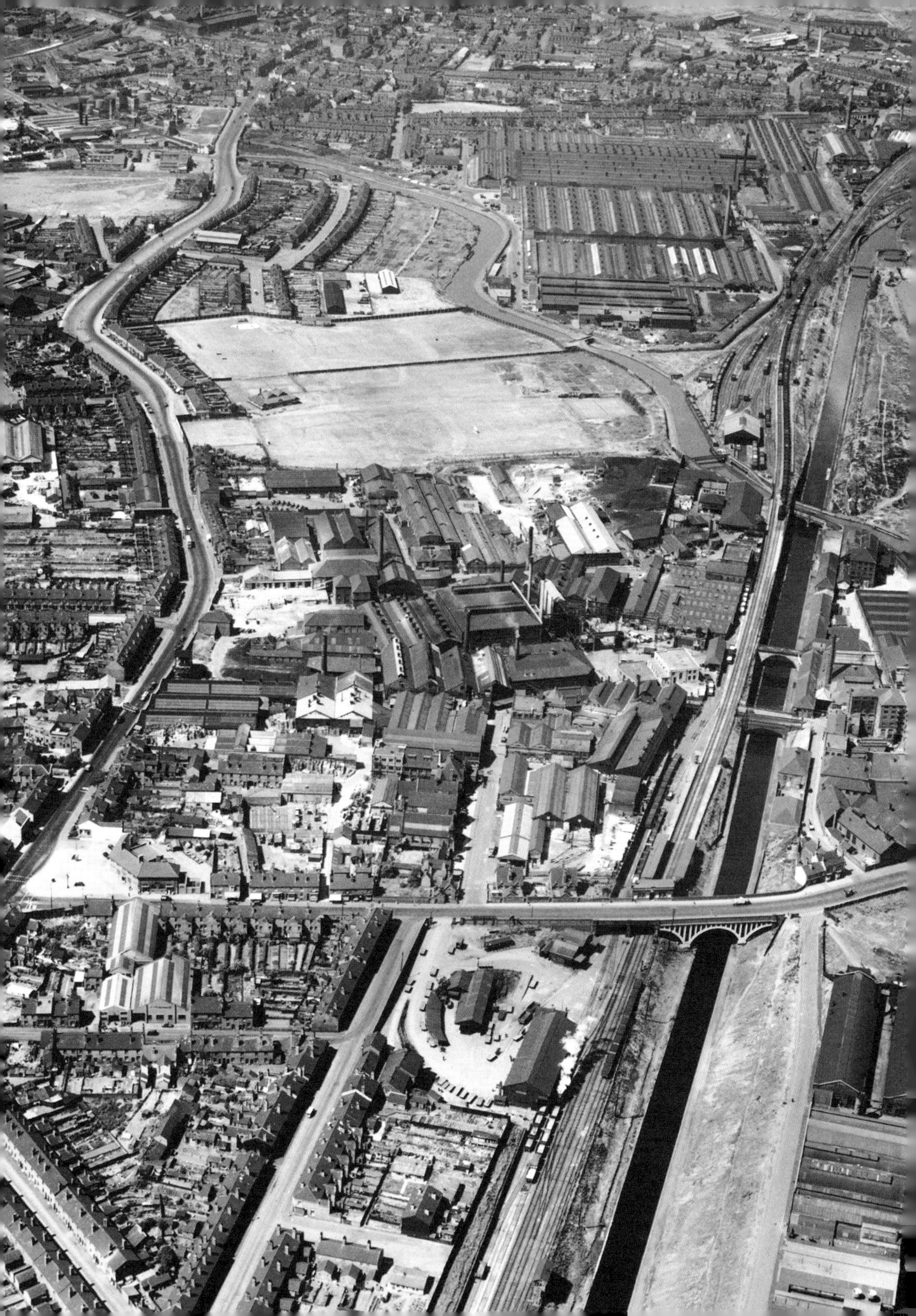

Brothers also have on display Third and Fourth Order optics, a type G Diaphone foghorn, drawings of the 1884 Eddystone along with the scale model, a gas buoy lens and lantern, optical glass, domestic glassware, rolled plate patterns, laboratory glassware (including an all glass interchangeable syringe), and Austinlite rotary switches.

Chances are also celebrated at a new exhibition space at Birmingham Museum of Science and Industry. At the Machinery Hall, the original 1873 light from the Longstone lighthouse provides the centre-piece attraction. In Smethwick, a 100th birthday party is held on their Recreation Ground, attended by over 7,500 people. In the weeks before, Arthur East, then an apprentice in the carpenter's shop, is kept busy turning the field into a fairground, building stalls and temporary toilets. One of his hobbies is model making, so he particularly enjoys building a 'rustic bridge' over the stream. On the day, there is a fancy dress parade for children, representing every country that ever needed a lighthouse, a 'Summer Girl' competition, running races, tug-of-wars, donkey rides, performances and comic turns from the Variety Section, a mass sing-along, exhibitions of handicraft, woodwork, metalwork, basketwork, flowers, photography and paintings. For the Grand Raffle, prizes include a television set and a refrigerator, though Lady Chance also finds herself presenting prizes of nylon stockings to gentlemen and strong liquor to youth. Fireworks conclude the day, set off by the laboratory technicians, with dancing in the Pavilion and on the green. That year over 2,200 people attend the Variety Section's panto, Aladdin. Cyril Harper reports for the in-house magazine Chance Comments: 'Andy Holland's arresting study of Abanazer was painted in grim and somber colours, while Taffy Llewellyn as the Dame was again a complete pantomime in himself, with the faithful George Woodcock stooging as Wishy Washee. Stanley Hinde's version of the Emperor was a satisfying mixture of quaint dignity and regal splendour.'

Over 1,000 people are using the facilities at the Recreation Ground, with some 600 signed up members. They have 16 acres of playing fields. It offers 2 hard courts for tennis, archery with first class equipment, angling 'in more attractive places than their local brook,' football, gardening, cricket, netball, golf, table tennis, bowling on a crown green. Unfortunately the green has been out of use due to a turf disease, but there is no ill-feeling; how groundsman Tom Dowd gets any grass to grow in this district is nobody's business. In the Pavilion there are music concerts held in the cinema room, a live performance by an instrumentalist, usually a pianist – they also play gramophone records. There are Old Tyme Dances on Mondays. A choral section rehearses Tuesdays. Alternative Saturdays offer dances hosted by the popular Roy Graham and His Rhythmaires. So popular that the floor wears out and soon has to be replaced.

Outside of the works, in 1953 there is controversy when Lee Lombard & His Orchestra perform at Smethwick's first Youth Ball at Thimblemill Baths. An unofficial 'bop' and 'jive' session at the ball so annoys devotees of conventional dancing that they are moved to write letters of protest. To call it a youth ball was misleading, writes Miss Brenda Jukes and Miss Roma Phillips: 'Perhaps they should inform the public it is to be a jazz session and not a ball, as was stated on the tickets.' The Master of Ceremonies, Sam Hill, a physical training and youth organiser, admits there was some jiving by about eight couples who 'established themselves near the band and started throwing themselves about as if a frenzy.' He says the band leader hoped to tire them out by acceding to their requests; even if that did not quite succeed, he feels there was very little interference with conventional dancing. He noted that there are certain undesirable clubs in and around Birmingham, frequented by flamboyantly-dressed coloured men where jive is practiced. It was his opinion that if you stopped jiving at well-conducted local dances 'you may well drive young folk to these clubs.'

Nevertheless, an anonymous letter to the local newspaper asks: 'Will one of your readers tell me is youth mad or am I? Most of the males had hairstyles that fully justified barbers' increased charges. Their flamboyant jackets hung below the armpits, while on their neckwear reclining females displayed their naked allurements. The girls, like most of Smethwick's teenagers on these occasions, looked charming. The band extracted (I will not say coaxed) from their instruments a noise that was reminiscent of stampeding cattle in the cowboy epics of my youth. Meanwhile, the devotees cavorted like demented witchdoctors seeking out the unfaithful, and occupying so much space that ordinary dancing was fraught with danger.' The Estates Committee of Smethwick Council decide that, in future, arrangements for the letting of their premises for dancing purposes must include a clause 'to prevent behaviour of dancers likely to interfere with the comfort of other dancers.'

No-one complains or worries about health & safety issues when the Gatekeeper at Chances, Walter Homer, performs with fire at the children's parties. He eats flames from a bundle of lighted tapers, thrilling the kids by licking white-hot iron bars and passing flames all over his body and down his throat. He says he has been doing this sort of thing for some 25 years now, winning challenges issued to him by the locals when he served in the Middle East with the Army. The children's events also offer conjurors and clowns, and showings of silent movie comedy classics.

Though there are less vacancies available, it seems everyone wants to work for Chances – surely it's a job for life. Look at the old timers. Harry F. Lloyd, foreman of the Mixing Plants, started work here on Boxing Day 1900. Arthur Potter was 13 years old in 1899 when he began; a long time ladler and now a glass crusher. Fred Stanley started as a labourer 51 years ago, removing soot from flues, and is still in the Optical Department making himself useful. His two sons, Henry and John, work in the Lighthouse Department. The Assistant Manager in Flat Glass, Bert Tandy, is about to retire; a keen supporter of the Recreation Club, he started in the Patent Plate warehouse in 1899, when his father was foreman of the Mixing Department and his uncles were blowers of coloured glass.

Many of the old timers that Sir Hugh Chance worked alongside have gone; Freddy Tickle for one, an overseas lighthouse erector, said to be the most traveled man in the works, from China to Peru, 'from Greenland's Icy Mountains to India's Coral strands.' He was, Sir Hugh recalls, an inveterate stutterer – 'when it is recorded he stuttered it was not merely stammering but a 100% stutter which rose to 200% when he became excited.' While superintending work on 'a cannibal island' he was said to be sure to carry a large revolver. Once he was approached by the local chief to accept office as King; he was so taken aback by the suggestion that he struggled to make himself understood – Sir Hugh reported that his words were 'so unintelligible that the Chief's offer was withdrawn in frustration.'

Then there's Chief Draughtsman Bill Richey, who retires after 63 years of service. Educated at Birmingham Arts & Technical School, he specialised in the design of dioptric apparatus and was responsible for many of the famous lights. Alan Taylor is a youngster starting out in the Drawing Office, going through a pile of ancient technical drawings and putting them in order, making sure everything is correct and legible. Old Bill walks up behind him, smoking his pipe, and casually says, 'What have you got there, lad?' Alan takes a closer look and realises he can see Bill's signature, alongside the date it was drawn – 1890. Bill then takes the time to explain it to him, and tells him all about the type of lighthouse it was going into. What an inspiration!

As a new generation comes into the factory, their sense of pride in the work is self-evident. The promotional brochure of 1951, *Mirror for Chance*, produced for the centenary, picks up on this, writing:

When a lad in his middle teens come straight from school to work at Spon Lane, he sees it all with a fresh, inquisitive eye, untroubled by history. And what he discovers is an allegiance to be proud of, a great range of skills to be mastered, a career with opportunities for a lifetime and community to which he henceforth belongs. Not a little. There are some 3,500 people working at Chances. And a high proportion have technical mastery of the kind which doesn't come after 12 months, or 12 years for that matter. At the moment of writing there are no less than 26 with more than 50 years service behind each of them were 50 years ago even these hands were new – and the future of the industry lies with young.

Kenneth Sutton-Jones is in Eritrea. He joins Chances as an apprentice engineer in 1937. It's a foggy morning when he arrives to find scores of cloth-capped men hurrying through the gate before the bell goes at 7.25 am. He is told this is the 5 minute warning before 'The Bull' blows, a bellowing steam whistle; by then you have to be clocked in. He is escorted through the works to the lighthouse department. There he given a file and told to dress a pile of castings by smoothing and removing the ribs and seams left by the foundry. At the end of his first day, all the foreman tells him is: 'Hold your file on the skew and don't make so much row!' As a southerner, he soon finds out that Black Country folk aren't afraid to give you their honest opinion. One morning, when he offers to do the tea run around the factory, they say, 'He ay too stook-oop to fetch the tay fer we.' Before long he feels quite at home, deciding: 'Each man was a specialist in some aspect but needed also a wide general knowledge. Ours was a highly prized factory, creating a product that had the function of aiding shipping and people and trade, and of saving lives. It was worthwhile and we knew it; and this ensured a wonderful cohesion and spirit of cooperation.'

He now works in Sales and is visiting 19 lighthouses wrecked in the war, assessing costs, from wild and desolate reefs to islands. He finds it is strange that there seems to be no open hatred of the Italians in that country. He travels by a local ship, a bit of a rust bucket; it is 'by no means the acme of comfort.' He sleeps on a camp bed on deck beneath unfamiliar stars. A rowing boat takes him as near as possible to a site and then he must wade through crabs, jellyfish and weed. At Sha'b Shakhs it is different; to reach this tower he must walk across an uninhabited waste, the heat over 90 degrees, a searing wind whipping across the desert, a blizzard of dust. He and the lighthouse engineer, Pietro Cassai, walk 21 miles before they find this iron tower, a lantern atop a metal tripod and central cylinder. Originally painted white with a black horizontal band, they find it in a sorry state. In all he travels some 700 miles along the coast visiting lights, with 26 other passengers on board, a cargo of quick lime, building timber and 4 cars. One night the bags of lime catch fire and have to be quickly tipped into the sea. He flies between Assab and Asmara over Mersa Fatma, a volcano under eruption, an awe-inspiring sight. He goes to Addis Ababa in an old Dakota via Gondar, then to Egypt and finally takes a flight to England with the Comet jet – which only takes 6 hours, the only way to travel in his opinion.

After leaving Holly Lodge Grammar School, Georgina Schlanker has been working at Chances for four years, first in sales, then the typing pool and now in the Optical Department. She attends Chance Technical College part time, aiming to achieve a shorthand speed of 80 words per minute and typing speed of 35 per minute. She enjoys cycling and youth hostelling. John Whitney studied commercial art and has worked on prototype lettering in the Globe Department, mould design in the Drawing Office, and silkscreen design for domestic ware and for the new line of Fiesta glass. He relaxes by playing trumpet with a 7-piece classical jazz band. Robert Beavon, a keen cricketer, is studying chemistry and hopes to enter management. Donald Bromwell is 19 and has served 3 years apprenticeship in the Carpenter's shop, maintaining the buildings alongside taking his City & Guilds Course. Diana Penn is a secretary with the Works Department – her father is a foreman with the Traffic Department. She is a keen ice skater. Lois Reeve came to Chances at the age of 15, commencing work on a teleprinter, now working as a telephonist. She likes dancing, walks and the cinema. After leaving Holly Lodge School, 18-year old Mary Hoole joins the Physics Laboratory as an apprentice physicist, one of the first girls to do so. 16-year old June Talbot works in the Drawing Office on tracing and general duties. She plays with the netball and tennis teams at the Recreation Club and likes drawing landscapes and animal studies.

Ronald Winspear has arrived from Weymouth, where he attended a public school. At the age of 18, he says he isn't really a scientist but is here to gain valuable industrial experience; he is far more interested in people than machines, spending a lot of his time studying the works of obscure philosophers. Reg Flavell is training as an engineer and is currently working in the Pyrometry Department. He plays football for Dudley Town Reserves, enjoys ballroom dancing, and collects gramophone records ranging from jazz pianist George Shearing to Debussy. 18-year old Gill Ward has been recruited to the Personnel Department. She is an active member of Warley

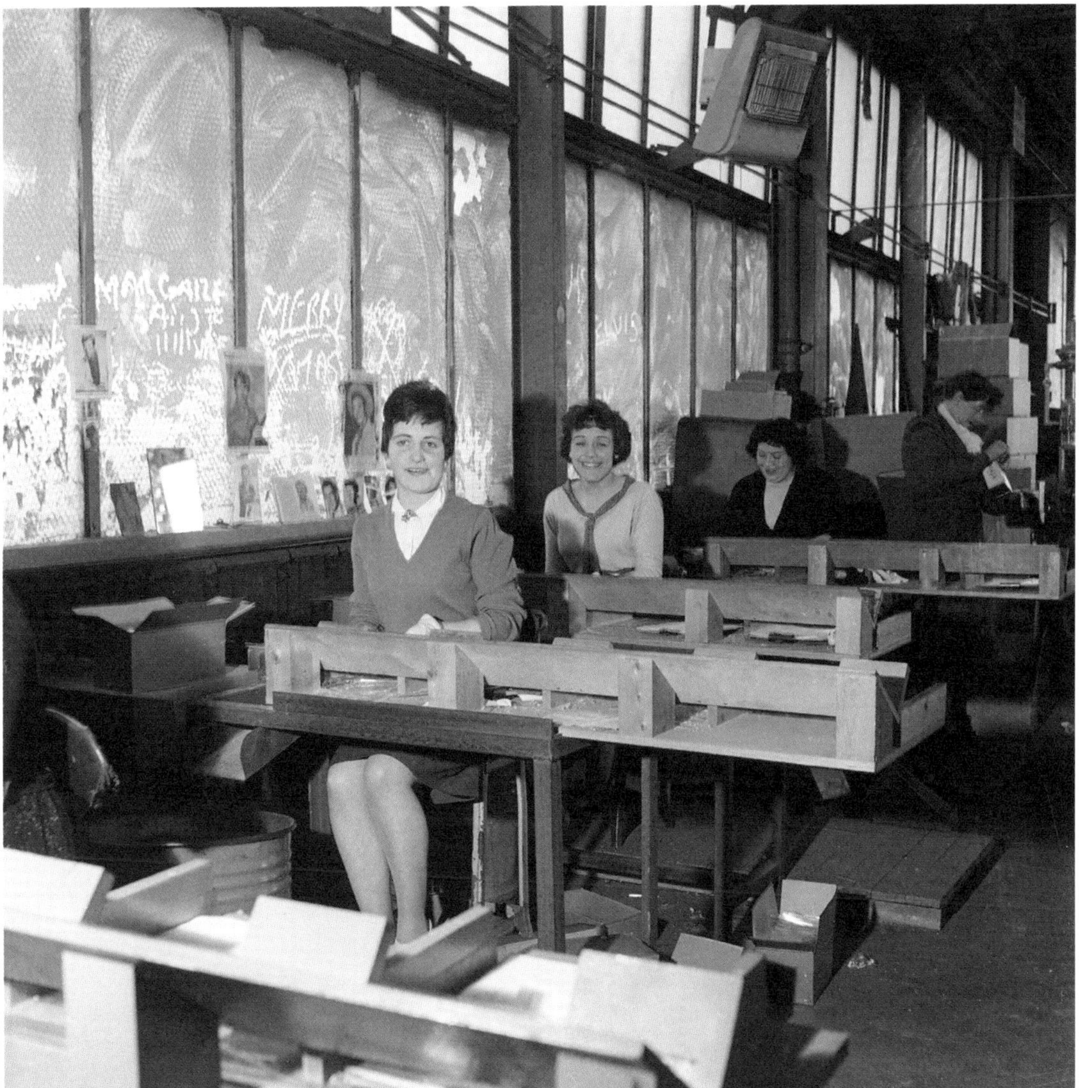

Woods Methodist Youth Club, and is a keen swimmer and hockey player. June Whitehouse has been working for five years as Dispatch Clerk and copy-typist in the Seven Storey. She represents the staff there on the Recreation Club Committee. She is also an organist at Bible Pattern Church in West Bromwich and is learning to drive. Edwin Cooper comes from Liberia in West Africa to work in the Drawing Office, then the Fitting and Machine Shops, part of a government sponsored scheme. He has acquired a liking for potatoes, having been invited to dinner with different families on Sundays. He has encountered nothing but friendly greetings, in his lodgings, at the works and at social events. Bengt Blomberg arrives from Sweden and George McPherson from Trinidad, both to undergo their training in the Lighthouse Department.

At the age of 14, Bill Matthews begins his working life work in the print room, near to the Sumo Pumps Drawing Office. He then undertakes a technical apprenticeship until the age of 21, with a day and evening at college, to specialise in mechanical engineering. He cycles to work each day, where he spends time in the machine shop, the lighthouse fitting shop, and finishes his training in the electrical section of the Lighthouse Drawing

Office. There he is tasked with doing the design for a new copper roof for the light at Great Orme Head, North Wales. He also works on designs for the lighthouse in Columbo where, as Ernie Barratt explains, they must drill deep into rock in order to install the automatic generating sets. He is given a drawing of the rock and told to work out how to fit all the rooms into it, no mean feat.

Bill is greatly appreciative of how Chances look after their young folk. They have a youth club, called the Malthouse, in a detached building opposite the glassworks entrance. They even organise holidays for the young people. He has been to Saints Bay in Guernsey, Saint Malo in Brittany, and Le Lavanadou on the Riviera. On that trip, 17 apprentices go for the two week industrial break, seeing the sights in Paris en route. They camp on the beach by the sea, with a perpetual chorus of crickets never ceasing day or night. Between 2 pm and 4 pm they sensibly keep out of the terrific sun. They are taken by coach to sightsee Cannes, Nice, Monte Carlo. The Riviera is a memorable experience, not least because they find they can buy boiled ham rolls; with the privations of food rationing still in place at home, he has never seen such a thing. So every single day they all go to the beach and spend their money on these tasty ham rolls.

Ray Drury began his 5-year apprenticeship in 1949 and has worked in the Blacksmiths Shop, the Sheet Metal and Steel Erection Shops, the Mill Wrights, the Machine Shop as well as the Lighthouse Department. He recalls: 'When you worked there you felt part of the company. You weren't just a number and that was the secret; you were made to feel important to the company and they reviewed you quietly, especially as an apprentice, but without making a big song and a dance about it. As an apprentice you looked at what the pensioners got, which seems a strange thing, but they used to get their Dog Licences paid, TV Licence paid, coal delivered at Christmas. Even though you might only be 18 years old and a long way away from retirement, this told you what the company was like and how it treated its people.' The youth club is open 7 nights a week for apprentices and then there's all the activitives at the Recreational Ground. He enjoys playing in the cricket team, year in year out. One day, Ray will become Chief Engineer, looking after the works, the buildings and all the plant, still feeling very much a part of the Chance Brothers club to the very end.

We are at the end of an era

Over 10,000 people leave Smethwick for the holiday fortnight. North Wales is their favourite location, though Weymouth also is becoming popular. Day-trippers head to Stourport by the River Severn, where many have a roughly built wooden bungalow. The Smethwick Telephone reports: 'One or two of them add an honest pound or two to their factory earnings by letting their shanties to holidaymakers in the summer months. And very nice too, if you are prepared to take your own blankets and put up with a lack of running water and somewhat primitive sanitation. Smethwick being what it is, you can't blame 'em for wanting to get away from it occasionally.'

Chemists report an exceptionally high demand for suntan creams and sunglasses. 'There has been a bumper holiday trade,' declares Mr A. M. Carr at West Smethwick. Photographic equipment, especially cameras and films, have been in great demand. But the drought is playing havoc with the maintenance of lawns, bowling greens and tennis courts, reports Mr Gammon, Chief Parks Superintendent of the town; the moisture loving dahlias have been set back but geraniums are thriving. Cresswells, the soft drinks manufacturer in the town, have been working until 10 at night as well as Saturdays and Sundays to satisfy the demand from thirsty customers. They are using an average of a ton of sugar a day – when their wartime ration had been 24 tons a year. In the hottest week they distribute 16,000 bottles locally. To satisfy this unprecedented demand their family size bottles, normally in 5 flavours, are only produced in one – the traditional lemonade, which was judged the best of all lemonades at the 1954 Brewers Exhibition, 'proof of its purity and flavour.'

Smethwick Council makes an announcement that in future their houses will be decorated to look like 'an artists dream' – 'or a surrealist nightmare' as one commentator has it. Dreary greens, browns, chocolate and cream colours are out of fashion, with pastel pinks, bright yellow and oranges now finding favour with the housing department. 'We're going to be daring,' says the Committee Chairman, Alderman Charles Spragg, claiming they will be repainting in a modern way. He also says that some 'brickbats instead of bouquets' are to be expected as clearly 'some people are afraid of colour.' He expresses greater concern about whether the new painting scheme will actually stand up to the weather. Soon they will proudly announce the opening of their 5,500th corporation built home – at No 1 Lennard Gardens, Foundry Lane, one of a block of 28 cottage-on-cottage two and

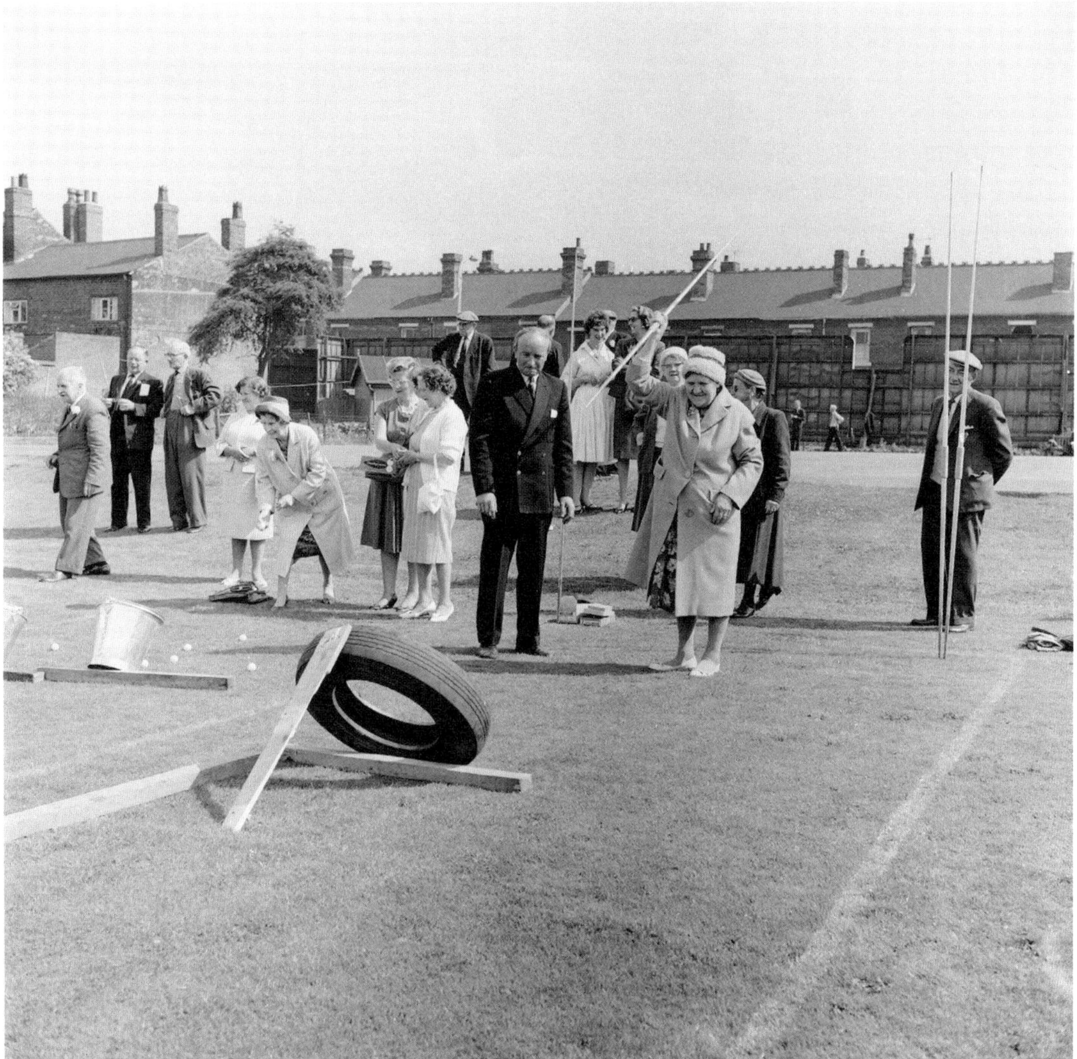

three bedroom type dwellings. The latest type of space-heating grate, fitted with gas ignition, is installed in the living room and supplies warm air to the kitchen. Each dwelling is wired for radio and television and has a detached brick-built pram and cycle store. Communal clothes drying rooms are provided on the third floor. Another landmark for civic pride.

John Fairhall, local reporter and a self-confessed southerner, says, 'There's a go ahead air about the town.' Having lived in seaside towns with rapidly changing populations he finds the neighbourliness of Smethwick people a pleasant change, though the accent is a shock. He admits it takes him nearly a fortnight before he can understand 'the sharp vowels that sounded like a wet finger being drawn across a window pane.' He sees a town which is 'a picture of dirt and grime and individualistic, friendly people, old and crowded housing areas and modern flats and schools. I shall remember a town under a haze of smoke where people work hard, play hard, and enjoy life to the full.'

A 19-year old German girl comes to Smethwick for three weeks to visit her pen pal. Rita Biervert speaks three languages and is training to be a law interpreter, so she spends time at Smethwick Quarter sessions. She likes the town but cannot get used to how tiny the houses are; back home nearly everyone lives in flats but they are more spacious. 'Smethwick people do not seem to show their emotions very much,' she says. 'In Cologne, if people feel like a good laugh or a good cry they go straight ahead, without worrying what other people think. Here nearly everyone's face seems to lack expression. I cannot understand why.'

There are other foreigners visiting the town. The first two students to visit this country from Communist Yugoslavia are Djordje Mandrino and his sister, Djurdjica, from Novi Sad, Serbia. They stay with Mr and Mrs Darby of Carnival Wines and Spirits Stores, having met their daughter Iris the previous year. They are taken on visits to factories and have a tour of the fire station. Apart from the friendliness of everyone, their main impression is of the large amount of traffic and the preponderance of white bread. They are particularly mystified by the popularity of ballroom dancing. 17-year-old Dieter Fischbach, from near Frankfurt, is the guest of Mr and Mrs Ball of Windmill Lane. Last year their son and daughter went to Germany, after striking up a pen pal friendship. Dieter sits in on lessons at Holly Lodge, enjoys swimming, tennis and putting, and goes to Blackpool with the family. He likes the town but not the litter – 'I was quite surprised at the way people throw litter all over the streets. Smethwick is very clean for an industrial town but the amount of litter is amazing.' Another German schoolboy, aged 15, arrives in the town after an adventurous 600 mile cycle trip from Rintlen, near Hameln. Bernd Klockhaus makes the journey alone to visit 16-year-old Desmond Hughes, a pupil at Holly Lodge. Their connectiom? Desmond's elder brother Gerald married a girl from Rintlen. Bernt has this to say about British people: 'They are very kind. Whenever I ask them something, they also repeat the answer so I can fully understand.' His only dislike? The many hills he has to cross on his way to Smethwick, which he found very tiring. While he is here, he enjoys swimming at Thimblemill Baths and plays golf – a game he is not at all familiar with.

There are some folk who are disappointed with life in Smethwick. Mrs Doreen Jagger of Merrivale Road plans to leave the Black Country for a new life in Port Elizabeth, South Africa. She tells the Smethwick Telephone, 'There are nothing but filthy dirty factories. Every morning, smells permeate everything in the house. You go out of the house and all you see are rows of houses all the same. There is no security. My husband is a welder and he has been redundant three times in 12 months. Social life is non-existent. In the evening there is nothing to do but listen in to the radio. It's unhealthy. My husband and my little girl both have bronchitis. I can't think of a single good thing to say for Smethwick.'

Perhaps she has a point. Only 20 people make the effort to attend a free demonstration of hypnotism, where Kenneth Spencer demonstrates his power, as assistant John Bassett lies across 2 chairs 'under his mesmeric control' while a member of the audience is invited to stand on his legs. The scene is captured by a local press photographer, who reports that Spencer had great difficulty in further persuading members of the audience to submit to similar experiments. Elsewhere, at the High Street Co-operative Rooms, only 21 people observe a minute's silence at Smethwick Communist Party's Stalin memorial meeting. A bowl of red tulips stands beneath a large portrait of Stalin. Two large banners are displayed, one grey with the Picasso dove of peace, the other the red banner of the local party. On display are various facsimiles of his writing. In defiance of local laws, they have chalked 'Stalin memo this way' on the sidewalks. Chairman of the local party, George Wesson, a clerk by profession, reads out some stanzas from Mayakovsky's epic poem on the death of Lenin. He criticises the Labour Member of Parliament for 'peddling ideas common to America and in the Tory Press.' His wife Edith speaks movingly of her visits to Czechoslovakia in 1947 and 1951. Riveting stuff. A collection taken during the meeting raises £3 12s 3d.

The Empire cinema is hired by an Indian welfare organisation, to show Indian films on Sunday nights for an experimental period of three months. 'Non-Indians are welcome to attend,' says Mr Hewitson, who runs the cinema, 'but they won't be able to understand them.' However, they will be also showing some documentaries with instructional features in English. He is more than happy to give it a trial as 'there is no doubt something should be done for these people in the way of entertainment.' By 1955, there is now a sufficiently large Indian community in the Spon Lane ward for the Conservative candidate in the council elections to send out a translation of his address.

At the Theatre Royal an American comedy – *The Moon is Blue* by H. Hugh Herbert – proves a hit. A film of the same name by Otto Preminger has recently fallen foul of the American censor because of 'an unacceptably light attitude towards seduction, illicit sex, chastity, and virginity.' The play is described as 'a comedy of innocence, for although its plot is sometimes audacious it is never offensive.' 21-year old Maureen Beck plays the enchanting heroine of 'fragrant innocence'; she will later be more familiar with locals when she appears on television in *Armchair Theatre*, *Emergency Ward 10* and *The Avengers*. Nearby in Dudley, the Hippodrome hope to attract a good audience from right across the Black Country for a one-off performance by Phyliss Dixey and her Peek-A-Boo show. She is touted as 'an expert in the art of striptease' with a class and charm that raises her above the standard of similar acts.

In 1954, Chance Comments magazine report on the deliberations of the Glass Age Development Committee. They have come up with a proposal for Southwark, London, called 'Skyport One.' The context is 2000 AD. As they put it: '40 odd years is far enough ahead to free the imagination from the immediate, and often ephemeral, limitations of today. But at the same time, the project is capable of being built today.' They imagine a city centre air terminal with a 500-foot high landing dock, set on top of three shafts, finned drums encased in an outer cylinder of glass. Inside these shafts high-speed lifts will link to the new Bakerloo underground station. The wings of the ground building will contain a transit hotel, an office block and a multi-story park for private aircraft and cars with 924 spaces. A sky-high revolving restaurant will also be encased with glass and titanium so the maximum amount of glass can be used – much of which will be coloured – 'the whole forming a magnificent example of the use of glass in a unique form.' The Committee expect that there will be vertical take off and landing aircraft and air-buses with 20-40 passengers, capable of traveling 300 miles, the air terminal to handle 720 passengers per hour. It's all a bit Dan Dare.

In April of this year the glassworks staff are told: 'There is such a close alliance between many of the glass products made by both Chances and Pilkingtons that very much closer association both in manufacture and in sales has become desirable and inevitable.' So the lighthouse and engineering section is sold off to J. Stone Holdings Ltd; a company that makes automatic generating plant, submersible pumps and foghorns, with works in Crawley and Deptford – it is renamed Stone-Chance. Managing Director John Raymond, who came to Spon Lane in 1938, says, 'I know Smethwick will be sad at losing its great lighthouse-making tradition. I am personally sorry to go because I've learnt to respect the Black Country and its craftsmen. We are gradually sorting out who will stay and who will go. It depends on fitting them into the new factory and if they are able to go.' Some will be offered new houses to rent in Crawley, not far from the new factory.

There are several hundred skilled workers in the works. By March 1956, only a handful remain. 'The huge workshops are shattered and silent,' reports a local newspaper. All that is left is an 11-foot high internal optic and rotating mechanism destined for Perrotan Island, India. The last lighthouse engineer, William F. Dimmock, tells a reporter: 'It's the last of the Mohicans for Smethwick.' Fred Ashley, a 47-year old optic fitter, works on this final optic, fitting 200 glass prisms into the solid brass holders. He doesn't like the idea of moving to a strange place, having worked here for 30 years and his father before him for 62 years in these same glassworks. He promised to stay on and finish this final job, but with his roots in Smethwick he doesn't like the idea of moving to a strange place. 'I'm more sad about the whole thing than I can say,' he tells the press.

In an unpublished memoir, Sir Hugh Chance writes: 'So after 100 years Chances gave up what had been an activity which had brought them credit and renown, contributed by a loyal Staff and by generations of skilled and hard working people... Only the bare bones of the one-time lighthouse works are there to remind us of the glories that have departed.' He stepped down as Chair of the company the previous year (though he remains a Director until 1964). Born in 1896, after service with the Royal Flying Corps and time as a POW, he obtained an engineering degree at Cambridge, joining the company in 1920, in charge of Rolled Plate, then becoming a Director in 1924. He has seen the best of times, the successes and struggles, and now faces the end of an era.

Where am yow agooen?

Dow tell me you ai never seen it, it's that bloomin' great finger of stone with the light atop. Right at the end of the land, there it stands, red an' white. Yow cor miss it. Tek the train down from Bilston, on the GWR to Bristol, change at Temple Meads for Dorchester, alight finally at Weymouth. Pretty as Weston-Super-Mare, warmer than Rhyll, farther on but better. The landlady's a cusser, gorra faerce like a fightin' cock. Dow get on her wrong side. Fish'n'chips on the esplanade, under the statue of King George the Third, who wet his feet here centuries ago. E's had a fresh coat of paint, looks a bit flushed to me. There's a bloke doin' sand sculptures, e's as brown as a berry. He meks mermaids and such like, not lighthouses. There's Michael Bentine and his flea circus at the Pavilion. Worra barmpot. Gordon Banks at Pontins, doin' Ali Baba magic tricks. Worra loff. Go to the wishing well at Upwey, mek a wish. I wished it wuz more interesting, wished we'd spot some real fairies and not just the ones in the gift shop on floral postcards or attached to pencil sharpeners. On rain days, and there's always some, we queue for the pictures, usually some steaming jungle thriller or western shoot-out that our Dad favours. *City Under the Sea* is showing, but the Pathecolor waters and underwater volcanoes fail to impress us when we have the majesty of the real thing off the Chesil, them waves starting in the Carolinas lurching our way, blowin' the cobwebs out our ears. Better still, tek a 'Mystery Tour' coach and likely end up at the Bill for a stroll, cucumber and crab sandwiches and another blast of fresh sea air. Not a werrit in the world on a grand day like this. We pay our homage to the glorious light, med to warn mariners of hazards, med to call 'em home safe. Med in the Black Country, though some sez Smerrick ai the Black Country. Well it certainly ai Brum.

It's the Shutdown puts us here, year after year, like homing pigeons, like we belong, but the Weymouth lads call us grockles. We dow care, we'm gooin' up in the werld. No caravan park in Evesham for us. We proudly pose for a photo by the tower, like we own it (in a way we do). Who else knows there's a bit of the Black Country here? My Nan sez there ai nowhere that dow 'ave our stuff, nowhere in the whole wide world our mighty werk ai gone. Bicycles in Iran, bridges in India, trains in Kowloon, tubes across the Americas and the lights here, there and everywhere, all med by our folk wi' skill and pride. Up the light, if the Keeper lets you in, you can see for miles and miles and miles and miles. Johnny Russell's older brother sez that The

Who must have been up 'ere and had a nosey around. He tries to hum the tune. He's a Mod and looks suspiciously at anyone wearing winklepickers. This autumn he'll be starting work in the foundry.

There's a lot of big white holes in the ground all over, from the quarrying. Dad sez there's some of that stone back in Windmill Lane, believe it or not, on that Bingo Hall what used to be the Gaumont – if yow look up at the top of the windows carved to look like the plumes of a peacock. That's from here, he sez. Ey ar kid, they med 'um to last in th'ode days. We sent 'em glass and they sent us some stone back. A lot of big broken lumps to climb over and in-between, the earth split open all about. Watch yer ankles.

It's a blustery place on the rocks today, everyone lined up like penguins having a look. Out there, a lot of wild waves. Some ferries heading to France. Some blokes with long rods, thinking about fishing in the coves if it calms. A crane lifts up a boat full of pots. There's not a bit of smoke in the air, no soot or nasty smells. As we say round our way, bostin' ai it?

LONGSTONE LIGHTHOUSE.
FARN ISLANDS. NORTHUMBERLAND.

ST. CATHERINE'S LIGHTHOUSE.
I.O.W.

PENDEEN LIGHTHOUSE.
CORNWALL.

PENNINIS LIGHTHOUSE,
ST MARY'S. SCILLY.

PORTLAND LIGHTHOUSE.
(PORTLAND BILL.)

SPURN HEAD LIGHTHOUSE
(OFF THE COAST OF YORKSHIRE)

DUNGENESS LIGHTHOUSE.

BISHOP ROCK LIGHTHOUSE.
SCILLY

SOUTH FORELAND LIGHTHOUSE.
ST. MARGARET'S BAY

LONGSHIPS LIGHTHOUSE.
LANDS END

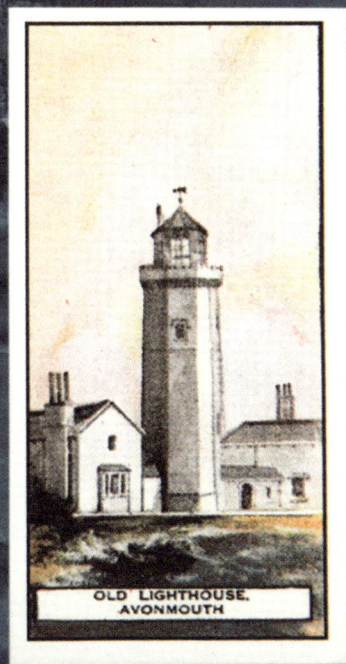
OLD LIGHTHOUSE.
AVONMOUTH

SKERRYVORE LIGHTHOUSE.
SCOTLAND

The lightkeepers

When building these great lighthouses, the Victorians may well have had words from the Sermon on the Mount in mind:

> *Everyone therefore who hears these words of mine, and does them, I will liken him to a wise man, who built his house on a rock. The rain came down, the floods came, and the winds blew, and beat on that house; and it didn't fall, for it was founded on the rock. Matthew 7:24–25.*

The lighthouse is seen as both a symbol of service to our fellow humans and of selfless sacrifice. 'Few people realise,' writes W. J. Lewis, 'what real hardship is endured by lighthouse keepers. They cannot imagine the solitude of a granite tower where the mournful moaning of the winds is often deafening, or the cramped living quarters, the uneventfulness, the isolation or the monotony of the work, of place and scenery.'

Lewis is a keeper between 1921 and 1965. He serves 33 years on rock stations, his first appointment on Bishop Rock in the Scilly Isles, the last at North Foreland. While there, in 1962, he wins first prize of £50 for a short story submitted to Readers Digest; this for a competition with the Seaman's Education Service, open to all British seafarers no matter what rank or rating. He calls his story *My most exciting experience*; it tells of how he spent several days, including Christmas Day, alone at Godrevy Island Lighthouse, off St Ives. With the other keeper suddenly taken ill and ashore, the weather closing in, he mans the station single-handed; no wireless or television, just the roaring seas and prey to his own imagination. He will later chronicle his life experiences in a book published in 1970, *My Ceaseless Vigil – My lonely years in the lighthouse service.*

After several weeks of instruction in the working and maintenance of the lights, electrics, batteries, the fog signal machinery and radio beacons, in Morse and semaphore, as well as a course in bakery, he begins his career. The light at Bishop Rock sits on top of a massive granite tower some 160 feet tall, with 10 floors, marking the eastern end of the North Atlantic shipping routes. Taking several years to build in such a precarious location, it was first lit in 1858. It required strengthening in 1887, when its height was increased, Chance Brothers fitting a new first order hyper-radial optic – actually two lenses, one atop the other.

Consider the typical duties of a Lighthouse Keeper around 1921. His priority daily duty is to keep the light on from sunset to sunrise. To ensure this each morning he has to: extinguish the lights, dismantle the burners and clean, then refill the lamps; carefully adjust the wicks of lamps, fit new wicks and trim when required; ensure that everything connected with the apparatus and lamps is perfectly clean and the lamp is ready for the evening; dust and polish the lenses and prisms; dust the framework and the apparatus; record in the log book weather and sea conditions every 3 hours, both day and night including observations of cloud shapes, sea conditions, wind direction, speed and barometric pressure – some 18 different categories, with the sea noted as one of the following: smooth, slight, moderate, rough, very rough, high, phenomenal (higher than 45 feet).

Other daily duties: ensure lantern curtains are in place to protect the lens from direct sunlight; clean the copper and brass fixtures of the apparatus; clean all the utensils used in the lantern and watch room; clean walls, floors and balconies, or galleries, of the lantern; sweep and dust the tower stairways, landings, doors, windows, recesses and passageways from the lantern room to the oils storage area.

Other regular duties: alternate the lamps inside the lens every 15 days; wash the lenses every 2 months with alcohol; polish lenses once a year with a special polish called rouge; once the routine connected with the light has been done, do repairs of a minor nature to the equipment and structure of the building; assist with relief supplies of coal, oil and water when necessary; keep grounds clean and orderly, painting of the tower (these last tasks for the land stations, there are no grounds outside Bishop Rock). One day in three he takes his turn to cook and cleans the kitchen.

Although times vary to some extent from station to station, the basic pattern over a three day period is as follows: Middle watch: 0000-0400, Morning watch: 0400-1200, Afternoon watch: 1200-2000, Evening watch 2000-1200. Lewis writes of how keeping watch has an extraordinary effect on his mind: 'One finds oneself in this way fully prepared to believe in wholly unreal happenings and beings, and any sound different from the usual lantern noises can cause a moment of terror.' However, there are no ghostly sightings reported at any of his duty stations, as there are reputed to be at South Stack, Point of Ayr or Souter. Rather he experiences some nights of 'infinite peace and beauty' and glorious sunrises.

In the quiet hours, he plays board and card games with his companions who, over the years, reveal an impressive range of hobbies – fretwork, copper and tin work, making wool, rag and rope mats, sketching, painting, silk-work, crocheting, knitting, and building model ships in a bottle. He remembers in particular the work of one Principal Keeper, who makes a full size bedspread

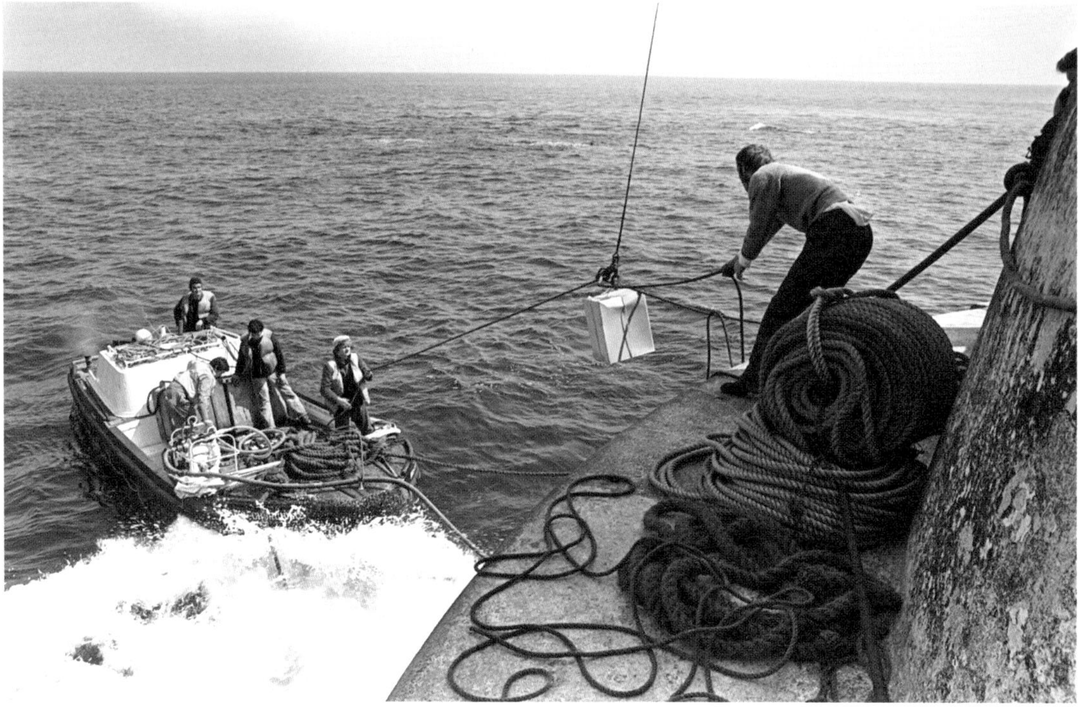

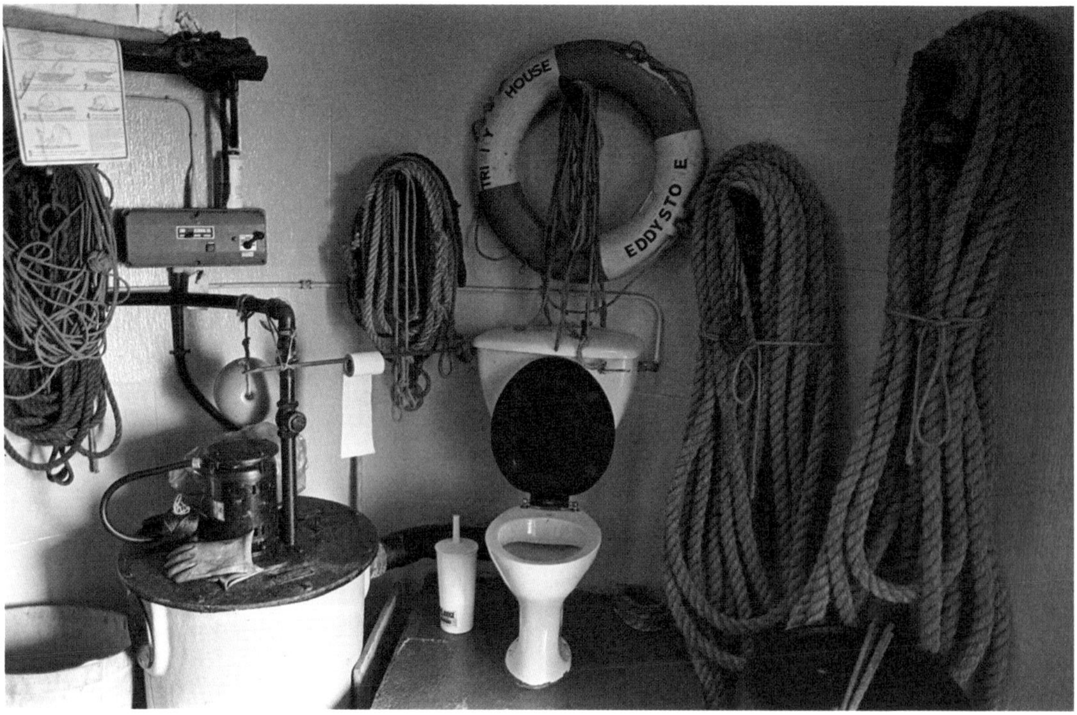
TRI
HOUSE
EDDYSTO E

with a pattern of fish, seaweed, shells and other marine life. Their supplies are supplemented by fishing. On the rock stations, between watches, Lewis studies the local marine life; when he is not based on a rock he records his fascination with geology, astrology, etymology and ornithology. One can get in a lot of reading as a lighthouse keeper, he says, as 'another day passed into oblivion, for seldom does anything memorable occur.'

In his lifetime of service, he has a fair share of bad storms, when the tower trembles with the impact of the waves, the cups on the dresser swinging back and forth, thick fogs closing in, condensation running down the walls. Confined to the tower for two months, sometimes longer if relief is delayed by the weather conditions, he notes: 'This is the sea, that vast expanse of blueish-green water, the ocean's graveyard which holds no carved headstone or boundary wall, the sea which is visited and admired not only for its construction but also for its powers of destruction.'

There are questions to be asked of a potential light keeper:
Have you been out into the sea in rough weather in a small boat?
Can you feel the strength and power of the sea?
Can your nerves hold?
Can you deal with a sense of loneliness?
Can you be self-reliant, patient, wash and cook for yourself,
mend mechanical things?
Can you have discussions instead of arguments?
Can you keep a civil tongue in your head?
Have you got a hobby or two to keep yourself busy with when
not on duty?
Can you be conscientious about taking your turn on watch,
no matter the time or day? Can you do so without complaint?
Can you make your own bread?
Then you might have it in you, young man.
PS. If you do not have a current interest in birds, you will without
doubt do so before too long, as you will be in close proximity to
guillemots and razorbills on stations such as Skokholm Island or
Bardsey Island.

Larry Walker is the last keeper at Portland Bill, his twenty third station. He has spent donkey's years with the Royal Marines and is looking for a job of consequence, a vocation like that of a policeman (which he has been for a time as a youngster) or a teacher. In 1970, he then sees a Trinity House advertisement for keepers – it is the 'salary currently under review' line that catches his attention. He applies and within 6 weeks he's in the service. It is, in some ways, an elite group; when he joins, there are some 172 keepers in England and Wales. It's a man's world for sure – when The Board of Trade in 1975 suggest to Trinity House that they should consider women keepers, they reply 'It is just not conceivable!'

Larry has relatives who've been at sea, and he himself has spent quite a bit of time on board ships. His wife is quite used to him being away, but with this job he will only be as far away as the coast. He begins as a Supernumerary Assistant Keeper, learning the trade by working at a series of different types of lights. SAK's are called upon to do duty at any lighthouse, covering for keepers who are sick or on leave, and they also do quarterly duty at rock stations.

He comes to the Bill from Bishop Rock. He also serves on the famous Eddystone. He remembers at the base of that tower, as you come down the steps, right opposite are three other steps painted red, on top of which is the toilet. He says, 'You could sit on the throne with the door open in front of you, a fine view out of the door looking towards Plymouth. On Bishop Rock we didn't have a loo. Under the lens table itself, we had a bucket with a wooden toilet seat on top. When you were finished, you took the bucket out the lantern door and you'd heave it, with the wind at your back of course. Away it goes. On Longships, they first had a yacht toilet installed in the early 1970s. They cut through the granite walls with a thermal lance, 14 feet of thickness, just to put the pipe in. Longships is a nasty one to be on. 110 feet high, rocks all round and with even just a little breeze a boat can't get near the place. When there's bad weather, the water coming up the sides of the tower, the fish waving at you as they fly past, your ears are popping, the barometer's all over the place. It's like rocking around on a Christmas tree.'

On Bishop Rock, in the winter of 1973-74, there are gale winds of 108 miles an hour, the seas coming up the sides, running right up the tower and the spray going over the lantern top. The tower is quivering. You're sitting in your chair and it's moving across the floor. Then a wave hits the tower so hard it knocks the relays out for the main lights and all goes black. The windows at the base of the tower leak and soon flood the bottom room, polluting all the fresh water tanks. On the last flight of stairs they find they are in water 8-9 feet deep. They exist on the juice out of tins of fruit until some five days later a helicopter manages to get out with some jerry cans of fresh water. Finally, a ship comes and pumps out all the seawater; they reline the tanks, neutralise the salt and refill them.

Despite the hardships, what he recalls most – and what he misses – is the comradeship with the lads. It was a small community, even more so when their wives and family are close by on a land station, as is the case with the Bill. Being a lighthouse keeper teaches you to be both tolerant and resilient. 'One of the prerequisites is a sense of humour,' he says. 'No point in being an extrovert or introvert, you have to be in the middle. You have to get on. Your job is the safety of the mariner. You don't know what nationality that ship is out there, but you're there to make sure he has a safe journey no matter where he is going. We are the sentinels of the sea. We are looking after the people out there. End of story.'

In 1996, Portland Bill goes automatic. He leaves as keeper but later returns as an adjutant, responsible for checking on the light if there is a problem, then reporting to Trinity House if they need to send an engineer from their control centre in Harwich. He says he will continue in this role as long as his legs can carry him up the steps. 'We all did a very worthwhile job. The lighthouses are still doing a grand job. Maybe in the future, there will be no need for them because of the advances in technology, but they're not going to take them away. They are not going to dismantle Portland Bill lighthouse. It's going to be here forever and more.'

Down Spon Lane, unforgettable

The men and women who work for Chances of Smethwick for the most part belong to Smethwick – many, indeed, to Spon Lane – and that through generations. These are Black Country folk, who would rather be less offended to be taken for Burmese than for Birminghamites. Their voices are distinct, their traditions permanent, their loyalties obstinate, and their sense of humour very much their own. The hobbies they choose are those of their countrymen. The skills they wield are a heritage. They name their children after minor prophets.
- from Mirror for Chance, 1951

In Smethwick, in the blacksmith's shop the sound of the hammers ringing out on the anvils. To Gary Watton, to watch them at work is pure magic. Sparks spit and fly as the glowing metal takes shape, a sharp hiss as it cools in the water bosh. Here they make and repair all kinds of machines for the glass factory, and they take pride in fabricating their own tools. Jack Hill introduces him to the strange looking equipment and tools – floor mandrels, swage blocks, tongs, scribers, flatters. One of the old hands, a fellow called Harry Homer, is ex-Navy and old enough to have served on battleships in the distant 1914-18 war. They are all big fellows and for a skinny young lad like Gary, who's 9 stone, that sledgehammer seems impossible to lift up. Harry just says to him, 'Pick it up lad, the Lord will send it down.'

Harry has an excellent bass singing voice and always breaks into song when one of his mates comes over from the machine shop. Together their voices rise up, the hammering subsides and the workers, even the foremen in their grey overalls with blue collars, pause for a few minutes of enjoyment. It's damn hard work but to Gary it seems a happy enough place. He learns there's a great pleasure in making something that you've done your very best to make. Before long he's sent off to the office of the Optical Department – staff are complaining about a gate which has a tendency to bang on the windows, so his task is to help Jack Hill put up some iron bars to protect the glass. There Gary spots a 15-year old trainee typist called Dorothy; before he knows it, Jack has gone straight in there to fix him up with a date and five years later – Bingo! – Gary and Dorothy get married.

There's a few love matches in the glassworks to celebrate. Alan and Joyce Taylor also meet at the factory. Joyce first works as a shorthand typist for the Education & Welfare Officer, Don Chapel. As an apprentice in the Drawing Office of the lighthouse works, Alan can always find a reason to visit Don's office. Joyce has all his records, so knows quite a bit about him already – for one thing, she thinks his timekeeping is horrible. They are both members at the Malthouse youth club, so there are opportunities to meet there. Something finally clicks and they start to date. Joyce contributes to Chance Comments magazine and will eventually become Welfare Officer. They have some trouble persuading women workers to wear overalls in the factory; eventually they decide to get different coloured overalls and warehouse coats. She recalls, 'If you said, 'You are going to wear this colour' the reply was usually 'I ai wearing that,' but if you give them the choice of the lilacs and the pinks, whatever they were, then ask them, 'Which colour do you like?' the answer was, 'Oh, I'll have that one, an' that one an' all.' It was safety clothing but as safety clothing went it was attractive. The idea was that they had the choice.' If someone has a moan or a grumble they go and see Joyce; whether she can sort it out for them or not is often 'in the lap of the Gods,' but they trust her to always have a bloomin' good try.

Alan starts as an office lad in the lighthouse works where the Drawing Office, on the second floor, is built onto the side of the main working area. A door opens onto a steel platform with some steps which go down into the workshops which are some 50-60 feet high. The view from here, effectively halfway up, is fantastic, especially when they test the lenses. He stands there as the optic rotates, the beams passing across in front of his eyes, a blinding flash; an unforgettable sight, quite overwhelming. Then on the shop floor itself, walking amongst the constructions towering above, with that powerful light casting, it's like a vision of fairyland. When testing goes on throughout the night, they illuminate the kitchens and living rooms in neighbouring streets. 'There's always a sense of wonderment,' he says. 'There might be two or three going at the same time. It was always a thrill to see.' As part of his training he spends 9 months in the Tool Room, then 6 months with the Tracing Section, where he sees how in earlier days the draughtsmen worked with ink directly onto cloth, embellishing their work by drawing human figures climbing ladders or standing in the lanterns. Now they work with pencil and paper, then employ tracers to make more durable linen copies when required. Most days, the draughtsmen walk over to the Pavilion on the Recreation Ground for their lunch break. Once a week one of the lads is sent to collect fish and chips from a shop on Oldbury Road. After lunch they usually have a kickabout with a football.

Another young apprentice, Dennis Arnold, watches his uncle, a glass blower, at work in the Globe Department. There's a teaser who first gets the molten glass off the end of the tube and gives it to his uncle, who puts it in a mould and blows. He notices how the glassblowers all have these huge malleable cheeks, which they can use to comic effect. He has another uncle, a Pot Setter in the Optical Department, where they manufacture the glass in big pots and he carefully places the pots into the furnaces. His Mother is there as well, at work in the Grinding Department on the engineering side. She grinds the glass that goes into the lighthouses. Dennis plays in the football team and he's also in the Fire Brigade. There's an incident when one of the furnaces erupt: 'There was molten glass just flowing out – it was like a river. We had to concentrate on trickling water onto the molten glass, to keep feeding the water onto it continuously until it got solid.' Dennis later goes to work in the Engineering Department for the Sumo Pump Section.

After the war ends, Arthur East leaves school at the age of 14 with plans to work on the railway, but his uncle sets him up with an interview at Chances and so he starts there as an apprentice carpenter. He is first sent to the gatehouse, where there's a post room with correspondence arriving twice a day, which needs someone to take round all the departments. This way, the young lad gets to see all the kinds of work being undertaken on the site. When you're that age, pretty green and wet behind the ears, you get given all the odd little jobs, fetching toast from the canteen for the Gatekeepers or polishing the big brass signpost that says Chance Brothers Glass (every morning and you better do that very well indeed or else). He later attends Chance Technical College one day a week to pass his City & Guilds exams; his ambition is to be a Foreman Carpenter. He soon finds he called on to make various sets for a production company who are making an educational film in the works. He has to repaint pipes 'the right colour' as instructed by the Art Director, build partitions to hide unsightly angles. The film starts with people digging in the old tunnels underneath one of the furnaces, unearthing a corpse of a Roman Centurion, the ghost of whom starts to tell the story of how they invented glassmaking.

A little artistic licence there perhaps, but Eddie Caine says there is supposed to be a ghost at Chances, only it's a gentleman with a stove-pipe top hat and not a galea helm. He never saw it when he worked the night shift, but there were stories. He says, 'Whatever manager was on nights they had to go up about 4.00 am and put the little furnaces on for the people that were coming in at 7.30 am and this one chap – a big chap, he'd been a Grenadier Guard – he came back and he was white as a sheet. I asked him what the matter was and he told me there was a ghost up there. He said it was walking along the wall. And he wouldn't go back up there again on his own. He always had to go with somebody after that. I went up there waiting, but I never seen anything... but I keep an open mind.' His brother Cyril agrees there were these rumours, though it was the rats the size of cats down the tunnels that bothered him more. 'The lighting wasn't good in those days,' he says. 'There was all sorts of things that could throw shadows from various places, like the furnaces and with the heat. The lighting was spasmodic so you can see where peoples imaginations might have come from.'

After the lighthouse and engineering section goes south, the Optical Division is eventually moved to St Asaph in North Wales. The Spon Lane site diminishes. Glass production will continue for some time in Smethwick as old processes are gradually phased out. The main products left are Rolled Plate and Fluorescent Tubing, though both Fiesta and microscope glass is still being made. The Rolled Plate Division ceases production in 1976, and the Tubing Division on the rest of the site finishes 5 years later, when the works completely close.

One apprentice who joined the company in 1949 has worked his way up the ladder to the position of Chief Engineer. And so it falls to Ray Drury to lock the factory gates for the last time, as the people of Smethwick suffer the impact of a decision made in the boardroom at St Helens. After production ceases, for 6 months he is the only one left, given the task to sell off all the machinery that he and his mates have spent a lifetime building. As he wanders the empty works, surrounded by memories of what they have achieved there, he thinks of all the jobs that have gone and what precious people these workers were. Some of those skills will be lost forever. He says: 'All those things we'd built and strived with and perfected, and altered and altered and altered. So many times we succeeded. We didn't fail all that often. We were proud of that. But at this stage it's all closing down and someone comes along and hits it with a sledgehammer and it goes in the skip. In comes the scrap man to take that lot away for a fiver and a goldfish. It broke my heart to be quite honest. It was soul destroying. I did weep.'

He had helped built equipment that went out all over the world, even though, as he likes to say, he himself never even got out the front door. He keeps the last piece of glass ever produced, turns out the lights, locks the doors behind him, sends the key onto Pilkingtons. It is a very sad occasion. 'They wanted me to go up there but I didn't want to. It wasn't my thing,' he says. 'I had a family down here, I'd got my Mother, I had my son in the best school in the area.' But still he feels so empty, feeling there is nothing beyond this moment. All that is left, these haunting thoughts.

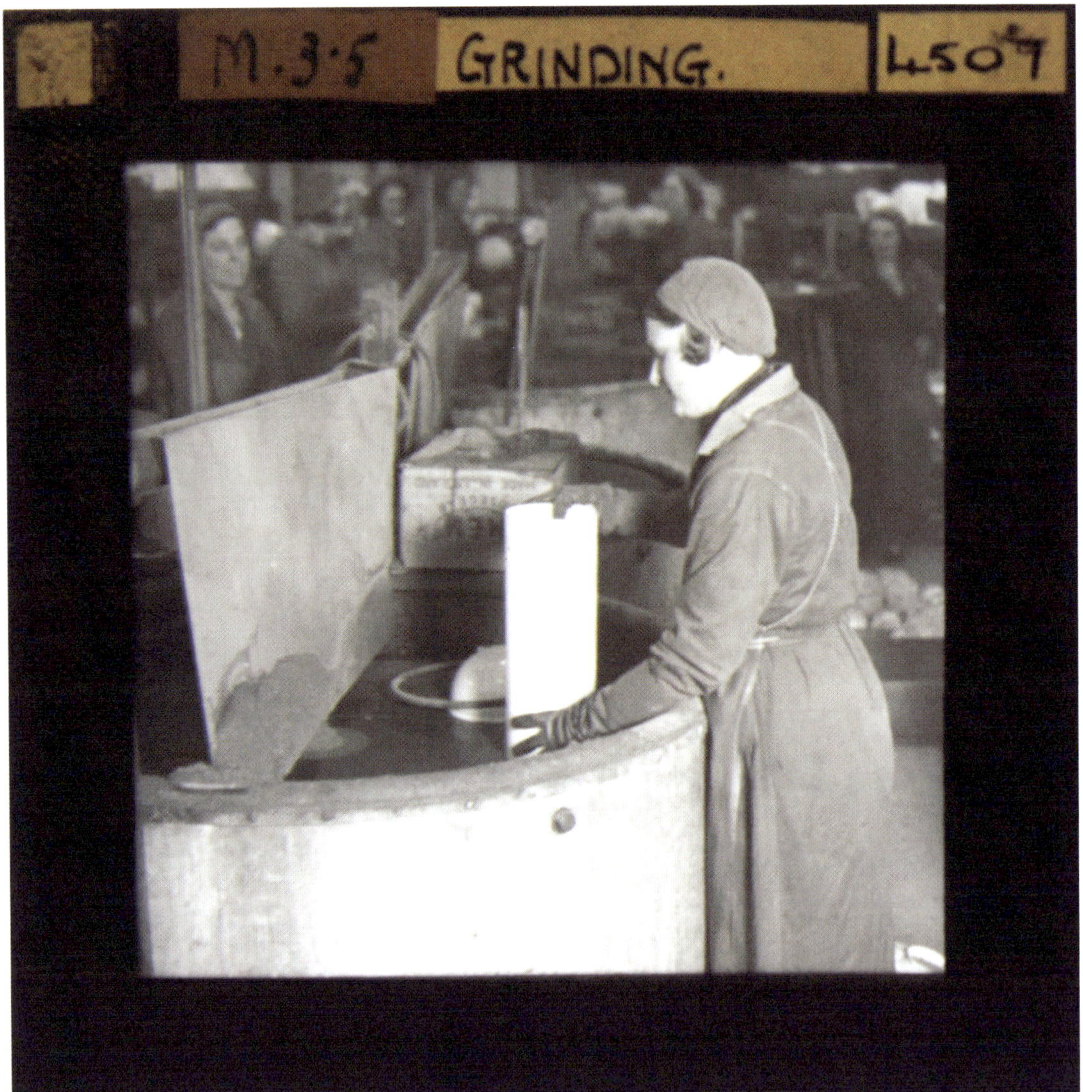
M.3.5
GRINDING.
4507

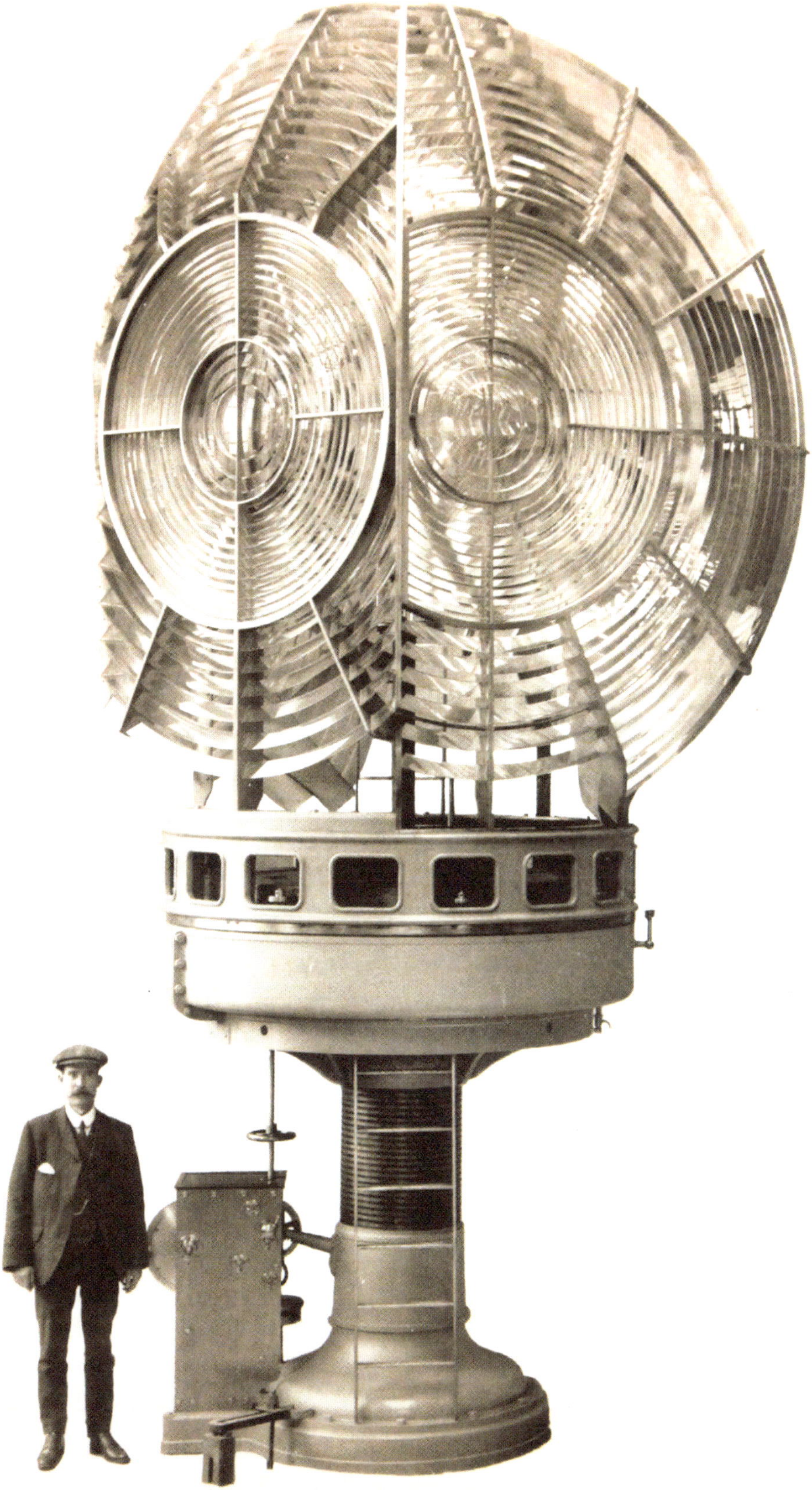

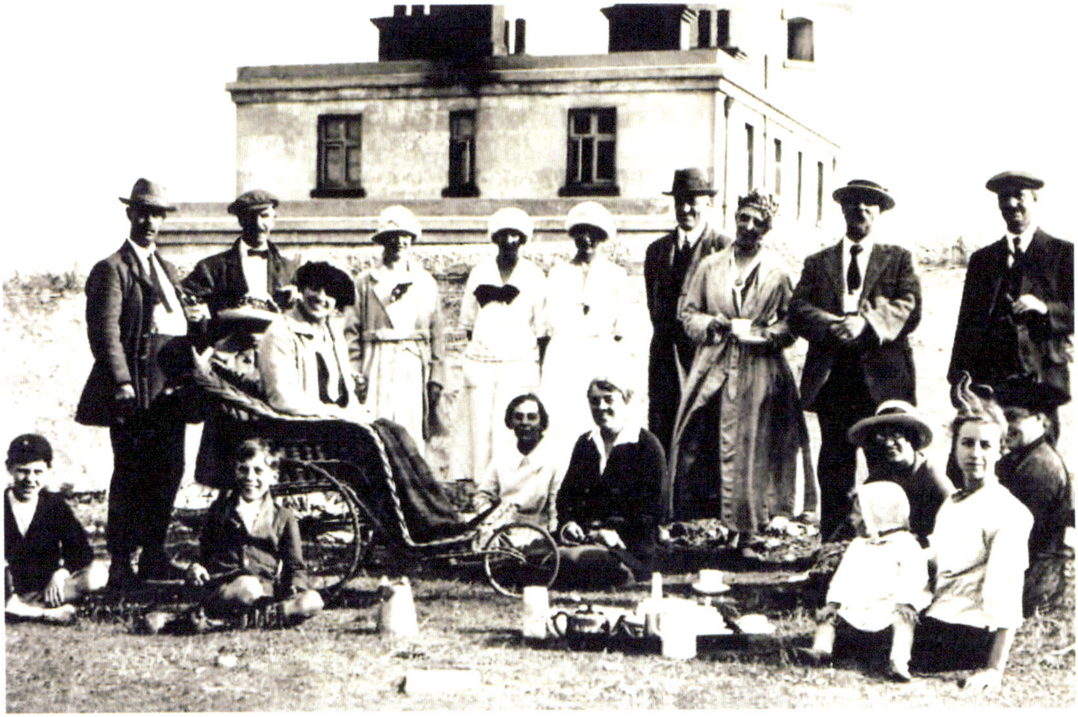

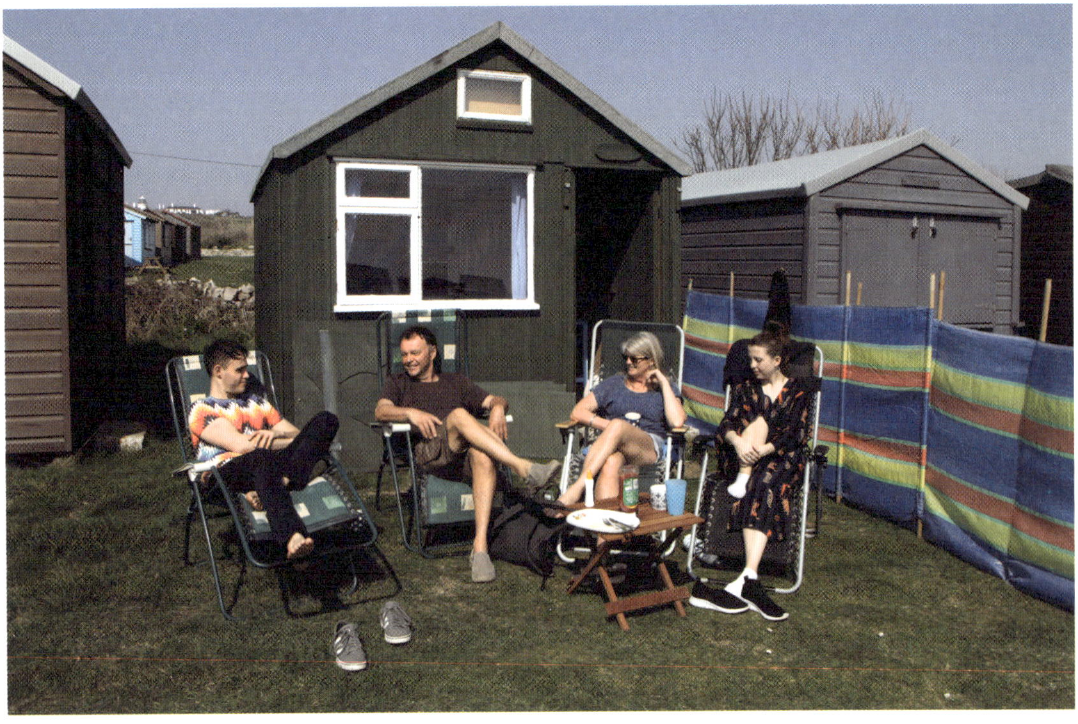

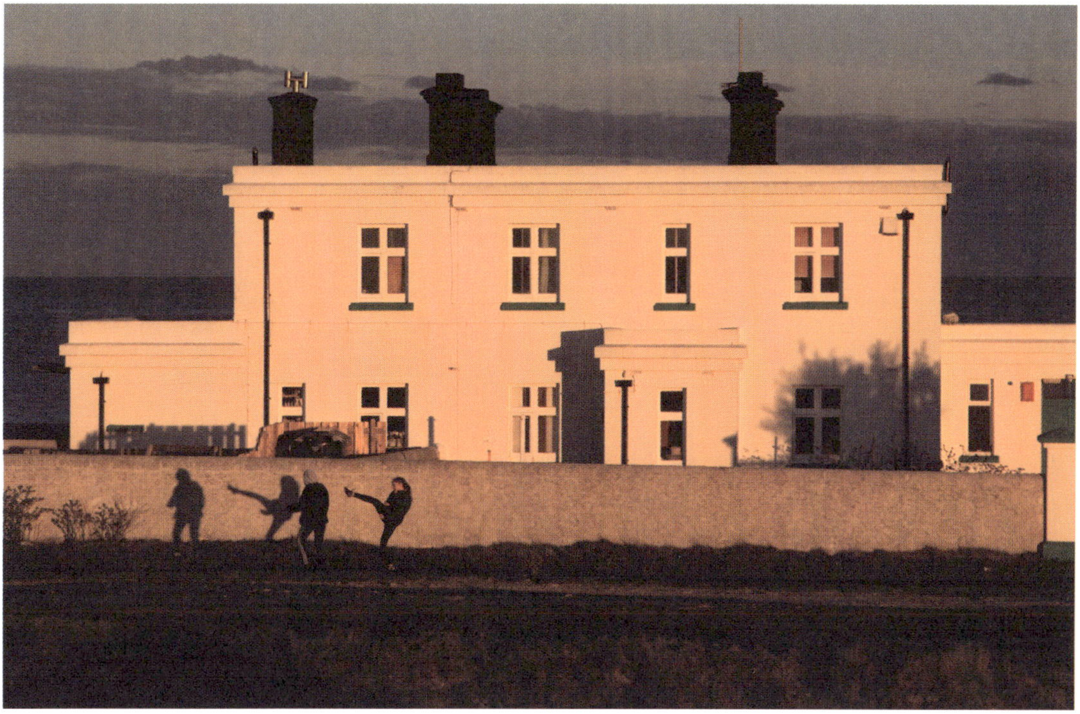

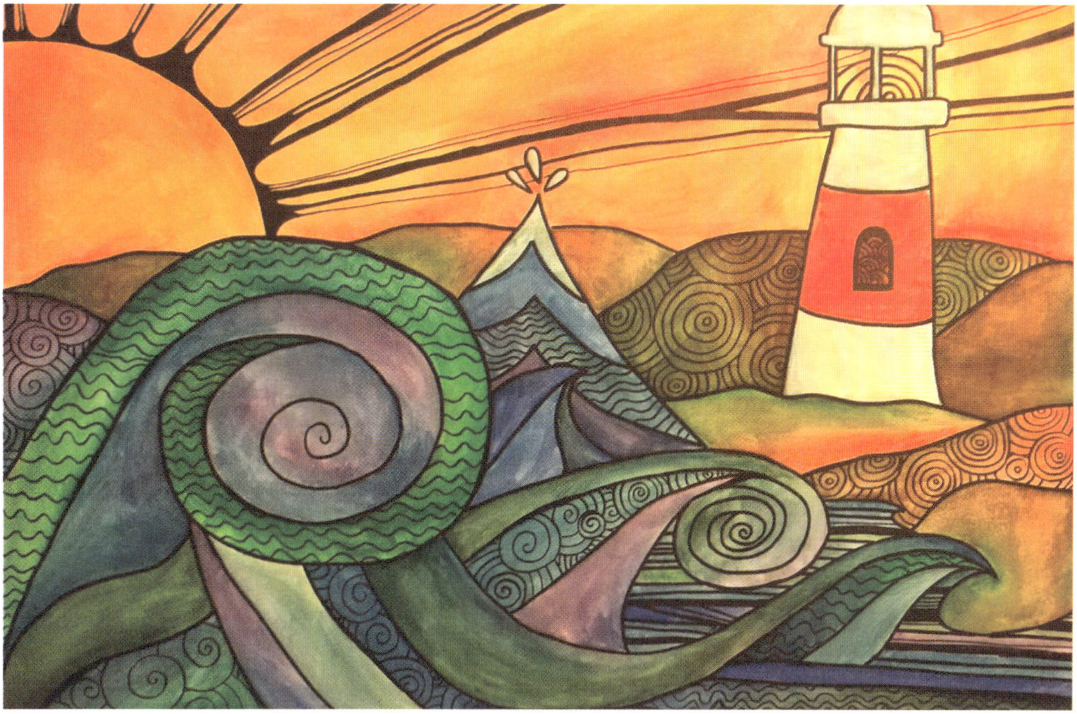

The Bill today

The car park is full on this bright spring day. There's a stiff breeze, as the tides flood up from the west. There are dog walkers, kite flyers, hikers, families well wrapped up, picnickers, a few mobility scooters, a fair amount of holidaymakers – accents from Liverpool, Sheffield, Birmingham, Poland and France among them – a few folk down at the sea edge looking to catch fish or crustaceans. Children run about the rocks exploring, climb down into crevasses, disappear, reappear. Climbers up the Pulpit Rock. No tombstoners today in sight, making their mad leaps into the sea.

The beach huts are strung out along the cliffs, some 280, mostly wooden constructions, some once made of corrugated iron, tar paper and driftwood used for generations by fishermen and local families, many neatly restored or rebuilt. Today, you can pick up one for around £30,000 – 'An opportunity to acquire a well presented beach hut in the popular location of Portland Bill. With the benefit of views over fields to the sea. Held on an annually renewable license' – and one of the nearby old coastguard cottages would set you back closer to £300,000. A couple discuss whether they have enough time on their parking ticket: 'A few hours round the island, then get the shopping, and we'll be back home by 7 pm to pop the tea the oven.'

Some will stay all day, sit and watch the sea, cameras and binoculars at the ready, spy a distant tanker or a fishing boat at work, kayakers casting off, a rigid hulled inflatable speeding by. The light is ever-changing. The Bill makes a natural destination for tour buses, ramblers and ornithologists, as it's the first point of landing for millions of migrating birds. Some locals still swim off the Bill a little further along in sheltered coves at low tide. People still tell you that Marie Stopes used to sunbathe naked on the rocks here.

For many, coming to the Bill has been a family tradition year on year, no matter what season. In the middle of winter on a stormy day, there are spectacular waves, and a warm refuge in the nearby Pulpit Inn. If you're looking for a place that is true British beauty, you might think this is it. The white signpost, which showed the mileage to different locations, where many people posed for pictures, has gone, much to the disappointment of some returnees, wishing to re-enact an old photograph. The Lobster Café is doing good business. A Japanese tourist eagerly orders what she assumes is their special. She ignores the crab sandwich platter, the homemade Smoked Haddock fishcake, the cheesy chips and the vegetarian wraps. 'I would like to try the Lobster Pot,' she says. The girl behind the counter looks bemused.

'Sorry?' The tourist tries once more, demonstrating with her hands, her companion joining in. 'Pot with lobster in it, please.' The girl finally answers, 'We don't have those.' The tourist points at the café sign then asks, 'Why are you called Lobster Pot with no pot with lobster?' 'Sorry, we don't have any lobster,' the girl reiterates. These tourists go away, somewhat crestfallen, perhaps debating the merit of its appearance in The Telegraph's list of their top 25 most charming seaside cafes – described there as 'unpretentious shellfish shack.' An alternative could be the Jailhouse Cafe, run by inmates up at the Verne Prison. Some stunning views to be had there, looking over where the Naval base once was (it closed in the 90s).

The Visitor Centre at the lighthouse is open. The fabulous Chance lens from 1905 is now replaced in autumn 2019 by a flashing LED lantern, finally exchanged for the latest in illumination technologies. The original lens is dissembled and reassembled in the base of the tower for future generations to view, where the air compressors and machinery for the old foghorn used to be, symbols of a seafaring nation. But no longer; 40 years ago we had 90,000 mariners, now down to 23,000, Britain owning just 0.8% of global shipping. With 95% of our imports coming by sea, we are just that small cantankerous island off the coast of Europe, and the English Channel remains, still there with all its hazards.

PORTLAND BILL 1971
CHANNEL ISLANDS 65
LAND'S END 189
TRYSULL 171
16TH. JULY 1971

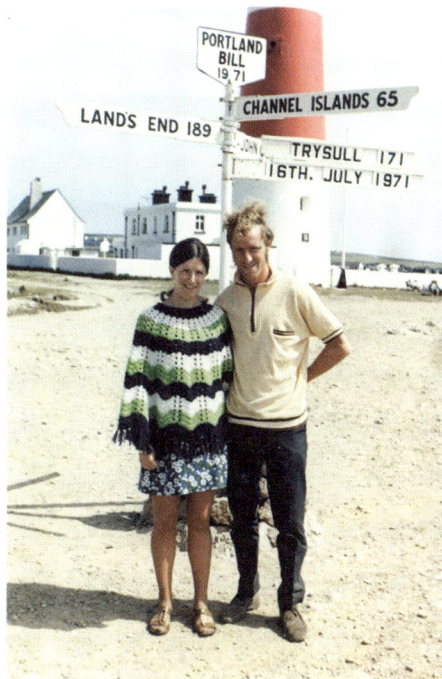

Well worth a visit!

One Saturday morning in 2019, members of the Chance family gather at the site of the former glassworks in Smethwick. Across generations, from across the globe, only a few have been here before. The oldest amongst them last came here as a young boy, just after the war, when he was invited to turn an 8 ton lighthouse lens with just his finger, sitting on its cushion of mercury. He barely recognises what is left. He looks up at the seven-storey building 'of 1847 vintage' and says, 'It must have seemed like a skyscraper at the time. I came to visit my father (Sir Hugh Chance) at work. It was before that monstrosity was built.' He is looking at the concrete ribbon of elevated motorway overhead, which dwarfs the site and covers the old canal. He went onto to train as an engineer at McGill University in Canada. His son and his grandson continue in the tradition. Must be something in the genes, they say. Some came here as teenagers in the early 1970s, watching in amazement as the molten fluorescent tubes poured out of nozzles, at the sheets of glass rolling along and cooling, being cracked into sheets, offcuts being broken up for reuse. When the works closed in 1981, over 150 years of glass production in Smethwick ended. Today, around 9 acres remain, a post-industrial space waiting to be re-imagined. Some buildings that stand along the canal side are reduced to only four walls. There are no furnaces left, though the tunnels beneath still exist. The south side of the site, where the lighthouse works once was, past the canal and rail line, is now a light industrial estate, along with a cash and carry and a gym. The road name leading into the estate offers the only clue to the past: Crystal Drive.

The old school house building is still there, with a blue plaque, alongside a war memorial to Chance workers. After posing for photographs here, the family explore the seven-storey together, a place that's easy to get lost in, amidst the discarded remnants of other tenants over the decades, the piles of old paperwork, ruined office furniture and scrapped equipment. On one floor, amongst the dust and detritus, they find a label for one of the many Chance off-shoot companies, and discuss whose signature the logo was originally based upon. They look at items donated to the Chance Glass Works Heritage Trust by a former worker, Alan Taylor, among them the glass menu for the centenary dinner and a small lens prism.

Henry Chance points up to the cupola on the roof, which once held the bell that rang out each morning to give 5 minutes notice before the beginning of work. 'If you weren't checked in by then, you'd be docked pay,' he says.

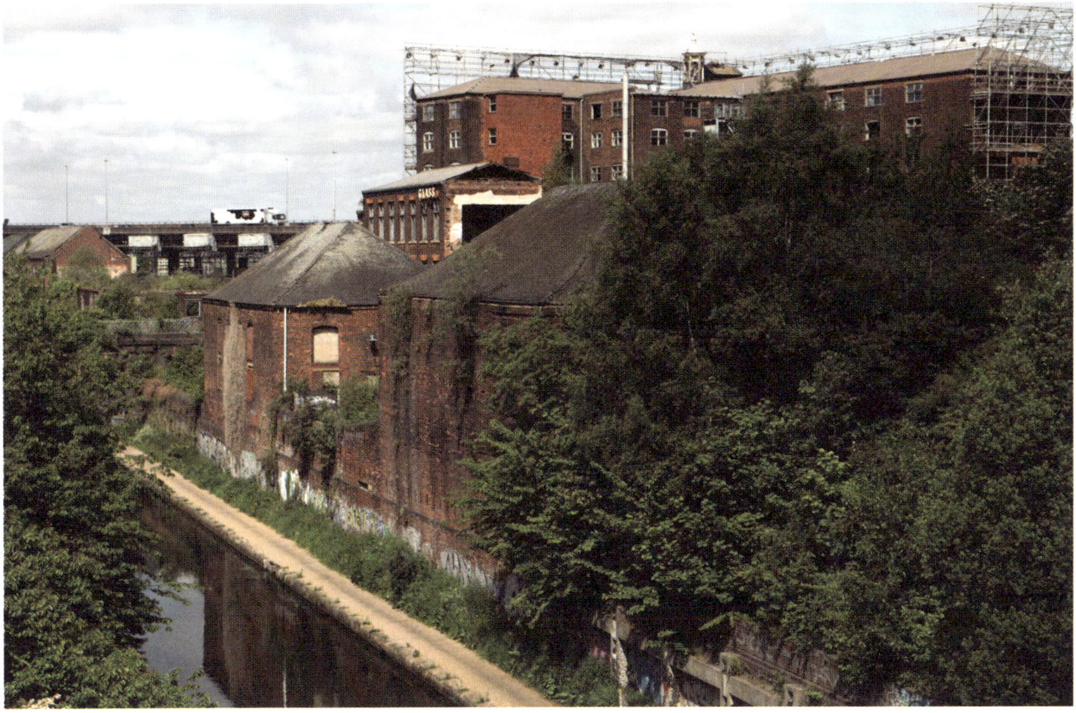

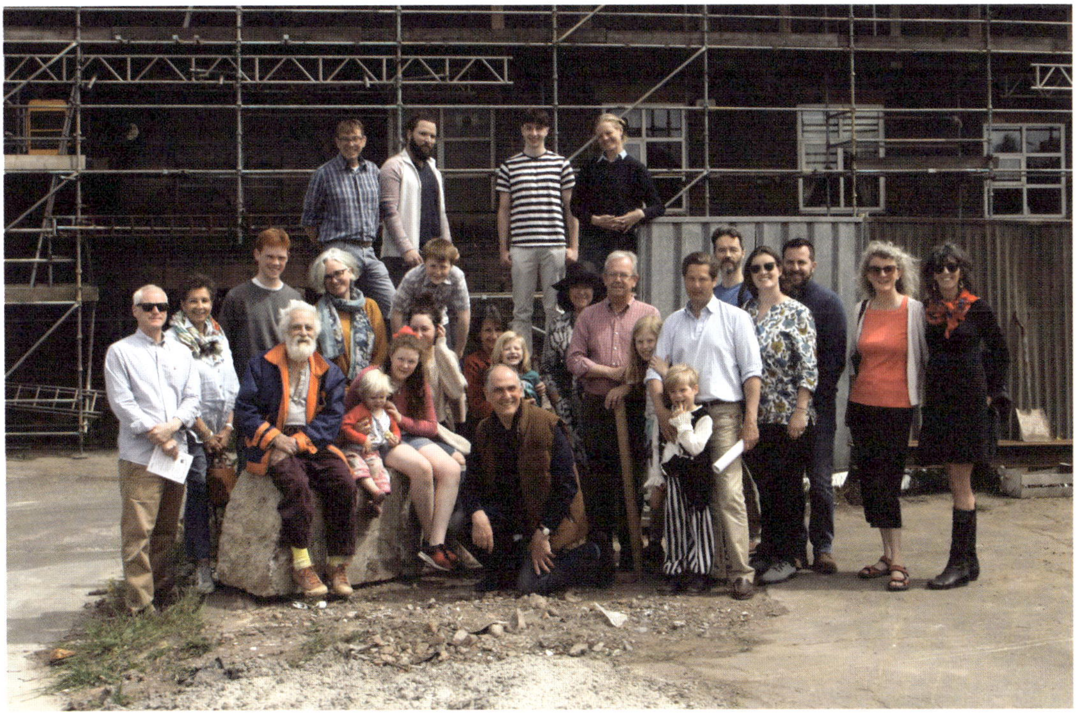

'No excuses.' The structure itself is not yet beyond repair. Mark Davies from the Trust, which was formed in 2015, outlines proposals to recreate the site into a mixed used development with due recognition of its history and glass making heritage. Several years ago, he had visited a lighthouse at Cape Leeuwin, on the most south-westerly point in Australia. He recalled standing at the top of the light: 'It was such a memorable moment, there I was gazing at a magnificent piece of engineering and finding out it was made here in Smethwick, by a company that I had never heard of before, yet I was born on the Rowley Hills, not few miles away.' He explains a recent project, where the tunnels beneath were mapped by OR3D, generously donating their time using 3D scanning technology to gain a better understanding of the archeological potential of the site, as part of research being undertaken with Historic England. They would also like to include a full size replica lighthouse, explains Henry, who volunteers time to help with the Trust. Here was a factory of skilled engineers, entrepreneurs and innovators, working with that remarkable phenomena – glass – which changed the conditions of society and life. Here is something worth remembering and celebrating.

Tim Chance is a marine engineer. Most of his working trips offer only brief glimpses of land; other than from nearshore craft he doesn't recollect seeing a lighthouse on the seas he's sailed. Both his grandfathers were engineers, as well as his father. He says, 'I was at first disappointed, as I'd thought at the time that I was cutting my own trail through life, and only later felt the link to family histories. I was proud when my son Brân chose to study (biomedical) engineering; but didn't miss an opportunity to tease him that he might have inherited the apparent paucity of originality.' This trip and reunion at Spon Lane reinforces the connection to those past Chance engineers.

Toby Chance first visited the Slangkop and Green Point lighthouses in Cape Town in 2005, and it was this that inspired him to write a book about the company. There he saw the shiny circular brass plate embossed with the words: 'Chance Brothers and Co. Limited, Lighthouse Engineers & Constructors, Near Birmingham.' His father, Sir Jeremy Chance, had worked tirelessly for some years to get the archives transferred from Pilkingtons at St Helens back to Smethwick. (This happened in 2007, an archive containing over 400 volumes, 100 boxes of drawings, and 500 boxes of other records such as minutes of meetings, agendas, orders and designs.) Toby recalls the moment at Slangkop: 'At night, watching the light revolve, it was almost like being in a dream. It was totally spectacular, watching these prisms cast their light some 30 miles out to sea. Imagine the intricate detail that went into setting those prisms, not to mention grinding them down. It is a work of art, no question about it. They are beautiful objects, which obviously have a utilitarian value, but nevertheless are gorgeous to look at.'

It's a very long way from the Black Country. Slangkop is a majestic iron lighthouse located near the village of Kommetjie, about 30 kilometres south of Cape Town. Equipped with a huge First Order quadruple flashing light (a lens quite similar to the one at Portland), it is painted white to stand out against the green background of the mountain behind. Prefabricated by Chance Brothers in 1914, due to the outbreak of war the light was not fully commissioned until 1919. It was put together using hand winches only. Each panel weighed around 500 kg and measured nearly five foot square. Particular attention was paid to the holding down bolts, as the commissioner specified a wind velocity of 60 lbs per square foot pressure, enough to resist a typhoon. It marks a dangerous promontory on the west side of the Cape Peninsula, facing the open Atlantic. At 115 feet high, it is the tallest in the southern hemisphere. Originally a 3-man station, it was automated in 1979, though there is still a Senior Light Keeper, who, amongst his other duties, still has to wash the windows.

Amazingly, in 2019, in the keeper's house there, tucked into the corner of a framed map of the coastline, is a faded postcard of Portland Bill, left by one visitor, who signed himself as Henry (another small coincidence). This Salmon Cameracolour postcard, which seems to date from the 90s, is fading from the sun. On the reverse, in tiny handwriting, Henry first thanks the light keeper for showing him around, even though it was a maintenance day. He writes: 'It was fascinating to see the rocket apparatus wagon. So much of our interesting equipment has been thrown away in the pursuit of modernisation. The phrase we have – "throwing the baby out with the bathwater" – springs to mind. Guard your heritage well!' He then shares the story of the lighthouse at the Bill, which he has visited. He tells of being fortunate to have made the journey on the RMS St Helena from Cape Town to Portland 'before she stopped making the voyage.' He concludes: 'Portland seems to be a place that rouses strong feelings – one way or the other! Some people hate it, but I love it. I find it an intriguing mix of drama and industry, with its rugged coast, 3 lights, & myriad footpaths that take you past quarries, prisons, windmills, and huge churches. The rest of Dorset is fascinating too. Well worth a visit!'

Keepers of the Light

ISBN 978-1-5272-4396-5

A book, film and instagram project by Geoff Broadway and Brendan Jackson. The artists would like to thank Sandwell Community History and Archives Service, Chances Glass Works Heritage Trust and b-side, Portland, for their help and support. Additional information: www. laundryline.co.uk/featured-projects/keepers-of-the-light

With thanks to the following individuals:

Rita Bailey; Ania Bas; Mary Bodfish; Janet Cartwright; Toby Chance, Henry Chance; Tim Chance; Ceri Davies; Mark Davies, Chance Glass Works Heritage Trust; Luke Dady, Archives Services Officer (Public Services), Dorset History Centre; Mike Fenton; Carol Houlden, Island of Portland Heritage Trust; Richard Flatley; Richard Franks; Nikki Fryer (extra big thankyou!); Kate Jackson; Fran Lockyer; Ken Lynham; Wendy Mahoney; Bill and Freda Matthews; Stuart Morris; Shirley Mitchell, Island of Portland Heritage Trust; Carola Northcott-Deacon; Magda Nowakowska; Kara Pearce, Neighbourhood Engagement Officer, Sandwell M.B.C.; Katy & Charlie Pascoe; Portland Bill Lighthouse Centre, Anne Hopkins, Giovanna Lewis, Kathy Smith; Alan Roberts, Amanda Wallwork, b-side; Graeme Rose; Sandwell Community History & Archives Service, Ian Gray, Maureen Waldron, Rory Powell; Smethwick Heritage Centre, Chris Sutton, Miriam Nori; Andy Straw; Alan Taylor family; Larry Walker; Gary and Dorothy Watton; Lucy Watkins, Portland Museum; Duncan Whitley.

Picture credits:

Cover image Portland Bill, 2019, Geoff Broadway.
p 1 Portland Bill lighthouse, 2019, Geoff Broadway.
pp 2/3 The sea off Portland, 2019, Geoff Broadway.
pp 4/5/8 Illustrations, Brendan Jackson; loss of the Lanona, Te Aroha News 24/3/1888.
pp 14/15 Pulpit Rock, courtesy of Ken Lynham; Lower light and Portland Bill under construction, 1905, courtesy of Stuart Morris.
p 19 Oldbury Road tram sheds, with Chance works in background, 1939, photographer Sam Parkes, Smethwick Photographic Society, courtesy of Sandwell Archives.
p 21 Blakemore Chemists, High Street, Smethwick, circa 1900, photographer unknown, courtesy of Sandwell Archives.
p 25 Publicity postcard of Theatre Royal, 1902-3, courtesy of Sandwell Archives.
p 29 Engineering workshop, Chances, early 1900s, courtesy of Sandwell Archives.
p 32 Chances, early 20th Century, photographer unknown, courtesy of Smethwick Heritage Centre.
p 33 Chances, early 20th Century, glass slide, photographer unknown, courtesy of Sandwell Archives.
p 38 Mr A. Perry in Chances yard with tower for Fort Cornwallis, Penang, 1882, courtesy of Sandwell Archives.
p 39 Lighthouse works, 1919, courtesy of Sandwell Archives.

p 40 Acetylene gas buoy, Portugal, circa 1923, courtesy of Sandwell Archives.

p 41 Buoys in lighthouse works, circa 1919, courtesy of Sandwell Archives.

p 42 The Isle of Portland from the mainland, 2019, Brendan Jackson.

p 44 Illustration, Brendan Jackson.

p 50 W.A. Attwooll postcard of Fortuneswell, circa 1905, courtesy of Portland Local & Family History Centre.

p 54 Convict postcard, circa 1900, courtesy of Portland Local & Family History Centre; Portland Bill postcard, circa 1910, courtesy of Ken Lynham.

p 56 Sailors and children, Portland, date unknown, D-DPA/1/PTD/235, published with permission of Dorset History Centre.

p 59 Castletown, 2019, with tattoo of swallow, Brendan Jackson.

pp 60/61 Chesil Beach, 2019, Geoff Broadway.

p 62 Family photographs, collection of the author.

p 67 Dorset Year Book, courtesy of Portland Local & Family History Centre.

p 69 Family Picnic, circa 1928, Portland Bill, Neina Hallet (Morris) on right, courtesy of Stuart Morris.

p 74 Dorset Daily Echo, August 1st, 1955.

p 76 Portland Bill, 1946, EAW002983 courtesy of britainfromabove.org.uk.

p 79 Top: 'The crew of first steam crane on Portland, 1920. This crew quarried the stone for the cenotaph in Whitehall, including my maternal grandfather Walter Slade (4th right). The quarry was opposite the Mermaid Inn at the bottom of Wakeham, now built over.' Bottom: 'Quarrymen working with Boy Lynham (4th left) and his brothers, also members of a Comben family working for Coombes Stone Co, Bumpers Lane, Wakeham. Photo staged to illustrate all the quarry tools and how they were used.' Both courtesy of Ken Lynham.

p 82 Lighthouse works, 1955, from left to right, Mr Neenan, D.P. Chowdhury, Frank Cartwright, courtesy of Janet Cartwright.

p 85 Chance Glass Works, circa late 50s, early 60s, photographer unknown, courtesy of Sandwell Archives.

p 87 Chance Glass Works, 1949, EAW024524 courtesy of britainfromabove.org.uk.

p 93 Chance Glass Works, circa late 50s, early 60s, photographer unknown, courtesy of Sandwell Archives.

p 94 Chance youth dance, circa late 50s, early 60s, photographer unknown, courtesy of Sandwell Archives.

p 97 Chance Recreation Ground, circa late 50s, early 60s, photographer unknown, courtesy of Sandwell Archives.

p 103 Weymouth, 1960s, collection of the author.

p 104 Wills Cigarettes Cards, 1926, collection of Smethwick Heritage Centre.

p 108 Relief at the Eddystone, circa 1978, Brendan Jackson.

p 111 Portland Bill fabric patch, 1960s, collection of the author.

p 116 Glass slide, Chances, circa 1920s, courtesy of Sandwell Archives.

p 117 Promotional photo of First Order lens, 1907, courtesy of Sandwell Archives.

p 118-119 Family group outside keeper's house, courtesy of Pam Wells, Portland Local & Family History Centre; former keeper's house, Graeme Rose and family at their hut, Portland Bill, 2019, Brendan Jackson; painting by Charlie Pascoe, 2019.

p 121 Portland Bill, 1971, courtesy of Wendy Mahoney.

p 123 Chances Glass Works and Chance family group, 2019, Brendan Jackson.

Reference:

Lighthouses: The Race to Illuminate the World, Toby Chance and Peter Williams, New Holland Publishers UK Ltd, 2008.

Chance Brothers: The French Connection, Rita Bailey, Smethwick Heritage Centre, 2019.

Mirror For Chance: Chance Brothers, Ltd, produced by Cecil D. Notley Advertising Ltd., London; printed by Thomas Forman Ltd., Nottingham, 1951.

Pharos: The Lighthouse Yesterday, Today and Tomorrow, Kenneth Sutton Jones, Michael Russell Publishing Ltd, 1985.

The Portland Year Book & Island record, 1905, reprinted Friends of Portland Museum, 2005.

Shipwrecks, Abbotsbury to Portland, Compiled by Peter Trim, Portland Heritage Trust, 1998.

Portland, An Illustrated History, Stuart Morris, Dovecote Press, 1996.

Portland Then and Now, Stuart Morris, Dovecote Press, 2006.

Portland Encylopedia, Rodney Legg, 1999.

Portlanders Tales, C. J. Samways, 1937.

Highways and Byways of Dorset, Sir Frederick Treves, Macmillan, 1906.

The Royal Navy: A History Since 1900, by Duncan Redford, Philip D. Grove, I.B.Tauris, 2014.

The Rise and Fall of Portland Naval Base, 1845-1995, Geoffrey Herbert Carter, Thesis for Doctor of Philosophy in Maritime History, Faculty of Arts, University of Exeter, 1998.

Long Voyage Home, True Stories from Britain's Twilight Maritime Year, Tim Madge, 1993.

Our Fighting Seamen, Lionel Yexley, Stanley Paul & Co., 1911.

Stokers – the lowest of the low? A Social History of Royal Navy Stokers 1850-1950, Tony Chamberlain, University of Exeter, PhD in History, 2013.

The English At the Seaside, Christopher Marsden, Collins, 1947.

The Countryside and How to Enjoy It, Odhams Press Ltd, Long Acre, London, 1948.

Ceaseless Vigil, My lonely years in the lighthouse service, W. J. Lewis, Harrap Co. Ltd, 1970.

Lighthouse, Tony Parker, London: Hutchinson, 1975.

The Story of our Lighthouses and Lightships, W.H. Davenport Adams, 1891.

Websites

www.intentional.com

www.brendanjackson.co.uk

www.geoffkirby.co.uk

www.portlandhistory.co.uk

www.stgeorgesreforne.co.uk

www.b-side.org.uk

www.portlandmuseum.co.uk

www.lighthousekeepers.co.uk

www.trinityhouse.co.uk

www.tobychance.com

www.blackcountryhistory.org

www.cgwht.org

Supported using public funding by

ARTS COUNCIL ENGLAND